A Roadmap towards Circular Economy of Albania

OECD
BETTER POLICIES FOR BETTER LIVES

Please cite this publication as:
OECD (2024), *A Roadmap towards Circular Economy of Albania*, OECD Publishing, Paris, https://doi.org/10.1787/8c970fdc-en.

ISBN 978-92-64-39996-9 (print)
ISBN 978-92-64-79623-2 (pdf)
ISBN 978-92-64-58521-8 (HTML)
ISBN 978-92-64-44317-4 (epub)

Photo credits: Cover © Edvin Rushitaj/Shutterstock.com.

Corrigenda to OECD publications may be found on line at: www.oecd.org/about/publishing/corrigenda.htm.

Foreword

In the pursuit of sustainable development and European Union (EU) and regional integration, Albania is actively confronting challenges stemming from climate change vulnerabilities, increased demand for raw materials and growing waste. The country is seeing rising momentum for the circular economy transition – one of the key pillars of the Green Agenda of the Western Balkans – and has recognised its significance in attaining national and regional environmental objectives.

The Ministry of Tourism and Environment is leading this transformative journey, notably through its newly established Directorate for Circular Economy. Despite commendable efforts and increased political and public focus on the circular economy, accompanied by the development of corresponding strategic documents, tangible outcomes of the circular transition remain incomplete. Insufficient awareness, scarce infrastructure, and limited financing options compounded by a lack of co-ordinated action collectively impede the effectiveness of current laws, policies, and overall initiatives, hindering the realisation of the full potential of the circular economy in Albania.

Guided by the OECD's circular economy methodology, this roadmap aims to assist the Albanian government in establishing a robust policy foundation for a successful circular transition. Drawing from a thorough diagnostic of Albania's circular economy landscape, the roadmap strategically incorporates current policy initiatives, and promotes strong alignment across the sectors, policy measures, and stakeholders involved in this transformative process. The in-depth analysis identifies a set of priority areas key for developing circular economy policies in Albania. Accompanied by a monitoring framework, the roadmap puts forward concrete policy recommendations for selected priority areas, including economic instruments, circular business models for small and medium-sized enterprises, and targeted solutions for plastics, with a focus on marine litter.

Integrating reforms for sustainable economic growth and implementing action plans for the green agenda are vital for fostering the production of sustainable products within the Common Regional Market. This approach, and the paradigm shift driven by circular economy principles, not only paves the way for access to the EU single market, but also underlines the commitment to environmental sustainability and economic resilience in alignment with EU standards.

The roadmap was produced by the OECD's South East Europe and Environment and Economy Integration Divisions, co-ordinated by the OECD South East Europe Regional Programme. It benefitted from inputs by a wide range of circular economy stakeholders, co-ordinated by the Ministry of Tourism and Environment of Albania. The work is co-funded by the European Union as part of the "EU Support to Competitiveness and Sustainability in the Western Balkans and Türkiye" project, which aims to reinforce economic governance and integration, and strengthen resilient and competitive markets.

Andreas Schaal

OECD Director for Global Relations and Co-operation and OECD Sherpa to the G7, the G20 and APEC

Mathieu Bousquet

Director for Thematic Support, Coordination of Policy and Financial Instruments, DG NEAR, European Commission

Acknowledgements

This roadmap was written under the guidance of Andreas Schaal, OECD Director for Global Relations and Co-operation and OECD Sherpa to the G7, the G20 and APEC; and Marzena Kisielewska, Head of the OECD South East Europe Division.

The work was led by Anita Richter, Deputy Head, and Jovana Pavlovic Djukic, Team Lead for Green Economy and Sustainability, both from the OECD South East Europe Division.

The principal authors are Jovana Pavlovic Djukic, Clémence Girin and Dafina Marashi (all from the OECD South East Europe Division) and Katarína Svatíková (OECD Environment and Economy Integration Division). The roadmap benefitted from substantive inputs and guidance from Peter Börkey (OECD Environment and Economy Integration Division). The lead review of the report was conducted by William Tompson (OECD Eurasia Division).

The OECD team extends its gratitude to the European Commission's Directorate-General Neighbourhood and Enlargement Negotiations (DG NEAR), particularly Sandrine Beauchamp, for her comprehensive support and valuable inputs during the development of the roadmap. The roadmap was also reviewed by the EU Delegation in Albania, notably by Jean-Noel Gangloff and Edvin Pacara.

Expert input and feedback were also collected from László Uhri from the Hungarian Ministry of Energy, and Rovena Preka from the Italian National Agency for New Technologies, Energy and Sustainable Economic Development, as well as other participants of the regional peer-to-peer learning platform on the circular economy, created by the OECD South East Europe Division.

The authors express their appreciation to Albania's national circular economy co-ordination team at the Ministry of Tourism and Environment, led by Sofjan Jaupaj, Director General for Economic Affairs and Support Services, and Elvana Ramaj, Director in Charge, Directorate of Circular Economy.

The stakeholder group comprised of government and non-government stakeholders, established by the Ministry of Tourism and Environment of Albania as part of the process of developing this roadmap, provided invaluable feedback on drafts of the roadmap, and contributed to the prioritisation of policy recommendations. The authors thank more than 70 participants from Albanian ministries, agencies, public bodies, private sector representatives, civil society, locally present international organisations and academia for their involvement.

Susan Rantalainen (OECD South East Europe Division) provided administrative and formatting support, Jennifer Allain (independent editor) edited and proofread the document, and Robert Akam (OECD Global Relations and Cooperation Directorate) provided communication guidance. Andrew Esson (independent graphic designer) developed the cover and graphic design of the communication materials for the report.

This roadmap has been produced with the financial assistance of the European Union.

Table of contents

FIGURES

TABLES

Acronyms and abbreviations

AIDA	Albanian Investment Development Agency
ALL	Albanian lek
CE	Circular economy
DMC	Domestic material consumption
DMI	Direct material input
DRS	Deposit-refund system
EEEOP	Environmental and Energy Efficiency Operational Programme
EPR	Extended producer responsibility
EU	European Union
EUR	Euro (currency)
GBP	Great British pound
GDP	Gross domestic product
GHG	Greenhouse gas
GPP	Green public procurement
HUF	Hungarian forint
NDC	Nationally Determined Contribution
NPIWM	National Plan for Integrated Waste Management
PAYT	Pay-as-you-throw
PE	Polyethylene
PET	Polyethylene terephthalate
PPP	Purchasing power parity
PRO	Producer responsibility organisation
SDG	Sustainable Development Goal
SME	Small and medium-sized enterprise
USD	United States dollar
VAT	Value-added tax
WB	Western Balkans

WEEE	Waste electrical and electronic equipment

Executive summary

This roadmap offers guidance to the Albanian government in laying a strong policy foundation for a successful circular transition. Informed by a comprehensive diagnostic of Albania's circular economy landscape, the roadmap outlines a set of key policy recommendations and promotes strong alignment across sectors, policy measures, and stakeholders involved in this transformative process.

There is a compelling case for a circular economy transition in Albania

Albania is increasingly embracing a circular economy, driven by its ambition to achieve sustainable economic growth, tackle persistent environmental challenges, and pursue regional and European Union (EU) integration.

Economic growth and heightened consumption are expected to increase the demand for raw materials in Albania, jeopardising its ability to relieve environmental pressures and hindering opportunities to enhance the competitiveness and resilience of its economy. Despite a doubling of resource productivity from 2016 to 2021, the economy still uses a relatively high volume of physical resources per unit of its gross domestic product. These trends amplify challenges in critical areas such as waste management, a significant threat to Albania's ecosystems, potentially compounding existing climate change vulnerabilities. Although waste generation is approximately 30% below the EU average, the trajectory of growing consumption implies a trend that could aggravate issues related to unmanaged and illegal landfills, widespread littering, and suboptimal waste management practices. These factors contribute to a low recycling rate of municipal waste (estimated at 17%), along with substantial marine pollution resulting from high rates of plastic leakage.

Albania's pursuit of EU membership and commitment to the Green Agenda for the Western Balkans serve as driving forces behind its endeavours in the circular economy. As the country progresses toward EU membership, it is strategically aligning its environmental policies and practices with established EU standards and regulations. Efforts to increase energy and resource efficiency, reduce waste, promote recycling, and implement eco-friendly initiatives are gaining traction, reflecting a collective commitment to mitigate environmental damage. Nevertheless, there is a need for these efforts to be intensified.

Albania needs a cohesive approach to guide it towards a circular economy, building the necessary infrastructure, raising awareness of the concept and providing financial impetus for an impactful transformation.

Proposed priority areas and key policy recommendations

The OECD analysis, based on a multi-criteria assessment and stakeholder consultations, identified three key areas where circular economy reforms could yield significant impact for Albania: **1) leveraging economic instruments for sustainable consumption and production; 2) supporting circular business models for small and medium-sized enterprises (SMEs); and 3) addressing the plastics value chain with a specific focus on marine litter**. This roadmap puts forward 35 policy recommendations, accompanied by a monitoring framework, intended to track their implementation across all priority areas. Identified policy measures across these areas can help enhance municipal waste management, contribute to developing a more sustainable tourism sector and foster greater understanding and awareness of the circular economy. Adopting and implementing these recommendations can also help Albania achieve its climate change mitigation objectives, as a significant share of greenhouse gas emissions is associated with materials production and consumption.

Stimulating sustainable consumption and production through the use of economic instruments

Economic instruments can help attain circular economy goals at a reduced economic cost, while simultaneously encouraging innovation. They incentivise change across the life cycle, targeting product design and production upstream, stimulating circular consumption patterns, and encouraging re-use and recycling downstream.

Key policy recommendations to strengthen the use of economic instruments include:

- Increase recycling and material recovery by implementing planned extended producer responsibility take-back schemes to increase the collection and recycling rates of specific waste streams (e.g. packaging, waste electrical and electronic equipment, batteries, and accumulators).
- Strengthen the incentives provided by fiscal instruments for the circular economy and implement new measures to address different stages in the product life cycle (e.g. landfill tax, materials taxes, household waste charge reforms).
- Gradually increase the use of green public procurement criteria as award criteria for a more circular supply of products and services.

Enabling the shift from traditional linear business models to circular business models for small and medium-sized enterprises

Circular business models can play a pivotal role in mitigating the environmental effects of material consumption. Given that SMEs constitute 99.8% of the firm population, helping SMEs design, adopt and scale up circular business models can contribute substantially to resource efficiency and environmental sustainability.

Key policy recommendations to support the adoption and scale circular business models include:

- Provide financial support for scaling up circular business models by introducing calls for SMEs within funding programmes and offer corresponding non-financial support.
- Establish and strengthen multi-stakeholder co-operation within and across value chains by establishing outlets for collaboration (e.g. circular economy business platforms, investor-entrepreneur matchmaking events).
- Raise SMEs' awareness and education on the circular economy through different engagement channels (e.g. communication campaigns, training programmes, administrative support).

Closing the plastics life cycle to keep materials in the loop and out of marine ecosystems

Plastic is a key material input in various sectors and is frequently disposed of in landfills at end-of-life or mismanaged. Low overall recycling rates and inadequate waste treatment significantly contribute to the leakage of plastic waste into the Mediterranean Sea. To shift away from primary plastics and boost recycling, Albania can leverage a set of targeted policy instruments, concentrating on critical applications.

Recommendations for a more circular plastics life cycle include:

- Close the plastics loop through increased recycling and better waste management by investing into infrastructure and other measures targeting plastic packaging waste (e.g. extended producer responsibility take-back schemes, deposit-refund systems).
- Shift demand from single-use plastics to alternatives and more reuse through a ban on single-use plastic products and targeted green public procurement.
- Curb virgin plastics use through design and production-related measures (e.g. eco-modulated fees, minimum recycled content requirements, taxes on plastics).
- Implement cross-cutting measures to raise awareness and educate authorities, businesses and households on preventing plastic waste and developing efforts to curb marine plastic litter.

1 Introduction

This chapter sets both the national and broader context of EU alignment for Albania's circular transition, offering insights into the objectives and scope of the circular economy roadmap. It also provides an overview of the concept of the circular economy and the momentum around its adoption in Albania.

Objectives and scope of the roadmap

The prime objective of this roadmap is to help the government of Albania set the policy foundations for its circular economy transition, strengthen inter-institutional co-ordination and stakeholder consultations, and drive the transformation in this regard. Building on a comprehensive diagnostic of the state-of-play of the circular economy in Albania, integrating ongoing policy efforts and aiming to create synergies between the different sectors, measures and actors involved in the circular economy, this roadmap presents key policy recommendations for three selected priority areas: 1) economic instruments (such as subsidies, taxes, charges or fiscal transfers); 2) circular business models for small and medium-sized enterprises (SMEs); and 3) plastics, with particular attention to marine litter. In addition to these selected priorities, three areas are tackled horizontally: 1) municipal waste management; 2) the tourism sector; and 3) knowledge and raising awareness of the circular economy among relevant stakeholders.

By integrating the measures outlined in this roadmap into its regulatory and policy framework, Albania can achieve a cohesive policy architecture. The implementation of the concrete measures will be key to enabling a transition to a circular and climate-neutral economy. Other direct and indirect benefits include: greater resource efficiency; improved waste management; reduced environmental pressure and the associated benefits for public health; improved material security; and increased industrial competitiveness and job creation. As these benefits are realised over time, they are expected to shape the long-term strategic direction and the institutional framework necessary for the transition to a circular economy, contributing positively to the fulfilment of national climate and other environmental goals.

The key elements of this roadmap that support the circular economy in Albania are:

- A rationale for the transition to a circular economy in general and within the Albanian context.
- A diagnostic presenting a comprehensive analysis of the state-of-play of the circular economy in key economic sectors, recent environmental developments and circular trends, and the existing policy landscape concerning the circular economy, highlighting the key policy gaps in Albania.
- A potential overarching vision and the roadmap's strategic goals and targets.
- An analysis of the three selected priority areas (economic instruments, circular business models and plastics), accompanied by key policy recommendations. Municipal waste management, the tourism sector, and knowledge and awareness of the circular economy are addressed as cross-cutting issues.
- A monitoring framework with a set of key indicators, based on European Union (EU) circular economy indicators, to support the implementation of the roadmap and measure progress towards achieving its objectives.

Context for the roadmap

Albania is proactively addressing the challenges posed by increasing climate change vulnerabilities, reliance on imported raw materials and increased waste, which have a significant impact on the country's pursuit of regional integration and alignment with the European Union. Enhancing competitiveness, promoting fair and equitable growth, decarbonising the economy, and safeguarding the environment are at the forefront of Albania's national policies.

Albania's commitment to sustainable development, reflected in its National Strategy for Development and Integration (2022-2030), is dependent on a successful shift towards circular economy principles, consistent with the United Nations Sustainable Development Goals (SDGs). Notably, Albania's path to sustainable development and EU integration requires an integrated approach to waste management, which is a crucial focus of its National Plan for Integrated Waste Management (2020-2035), to gradually transition from a linear waste model to a circular approach promoting reuse and recycling.

While Albania has yet to establish a comprehensive framework for environmental protection which extends beyond climate change mitigation, the National Strategy for Climate Change (2020-2030) concentrates on strengthening institutional capacity to reduce greenhouse gas (GHG) emissions, aligning with the EU climate framework and the goals of the Paris Agreement. Additionally, environmental considerations are increasingly being taken into account in industry-relevant policies. This is, for example, reflected in the Business Investment and Development Strategy (2021-2027), which focuses on promoting green investments, changes in the supply chain for more circular products and services, and empowering eco-innovation in key economic sectors.

Key institutions in Albania have acknowledged the significance of a circular transition in achieving national and regional development objectives. The Ministry of Tourism and Environment is spearheading this shift, notably through its newly established Directorate for Circular Economy. The cross-cutting nature of the circular transition requires whole-of-government involvement in the formulation and implementation of circular economy policies. Hence, other institutions like the Ministry of Finance and Economy, the Ministry of Infrastructure and Energy, and the National Environmental Agency equally contribute to this transformative effort.

However, concrete advancements in the circular economy in Albania have been limited so far. Some of the main challenges in this regard are the low awareness on circular economy concepts among citizens and businesses,[1] the lack of adequate infrastructure, and the limited financing options for businesses. Moreover, existing efforts are rather fragmented, lacking a unified and co-ordinated approach. This lack of concerted action remains a key impediment for transitioning to a circular economy in Albania and the main rationale for the development of this roadmap.

Overview of the circular economy

The circular economy concept

Growing concerns surrounding environmental issues such as climate change, acidification, eutrophication and intensive land use have drawn global attention to the ever-rising levels of material extraction and consumption. This acknowledgment underscores the significance of the circular economy concept, which marks a fundamental departure from the traditional linear economic model of "take-make-dispose" and offers a promising approach to mitigating environmental pollution.

In a circular economy, goods and services are intentionally designed, produced and consumed to minimise the use of material resources. This approach champions key principles like waste reduction along the complete product life cycle, material recovery from waste streams for recycling or reuse, the extension of product life cycles, durability, and the exploration of potential within the sharing and services economy. It advocates for the repair, reuse and recycling of materials and products, all in the pursuit of creating a regenerative closed-loop system.

More specifically, a circular economy transforms the flows of products and materials through three key mechanisms (McCarthy, Dellink and Bibas, 2018[1]):

- **Closing resource loops** through the substitution of secondary materials and second-hand, repaired or remanufactured products in place of their virgin equivalents.
- **Slowing resource loops** through the emergence of products which remain in the economy for longer, usually due to more durable product design.
- **Narrowing resource flows** through more efficient use of natural resources, materials and products, including the development and dissemination of new production technologies, increased use of existing assets and shifts in consumption behaviour.

Transitioning to a circular economy promises numerous benefits. It significantly enhances resource efficiency and fosters the sustainable management of materials, effectively curbing resource depletion and reducing ecosystem degradation. Circular economy practices also contribute to lowering the carbon footprint associated with economic activities, by minimising energy-intensive processes in raw material extraction and processing, reducing the frequency of production and disposal, and curbing waste emissions. Furthermore, these practices foster innovation and sustainable design, amplifying their positive environmental impact. The advantages of this shift range from a substantial reduction in GHG emissions and the creation of new employment opportunities to decreased reliance on scarce resources. Not only does the circular economy prioritise environmental sustainability, but it also fortifies economic resilience and encourages innovation for more sustainable production and consumption practices.

The circular economy concept has gained widespread acceptance, finding its place in national and international policy making, civil society, and the business sector. However, it is essential to note that there is no universal definition or approach to it. Instead, policies and initiatives are tailored to align with the specific objectives of governments seeking a transition toward a resource-efficient circular economy.

Enhancing resource efficiency and advancing the transition to a circular economy are integral components of green growth, and their significance is widely recognised in comprehensive environmental and economic policies. Several international organisations are actively engaged in promoting the circular economy. For instance, the OECD has established a Circular Economy Policy Framework, offering guidance to its member countries in their transition towards circularity. The United Nations promotes sustainable consumption and production through the SDGs, particularly SDG 12. Additionally, the Plastic Waste Partnership, led by the United Nations Environment Programme, tackles global plastic pollution through circular solutions. The World Economic Forum's Circular Economy Initiative champions circular business practices, while the G7 Alliance on Resource Efficiency advocates for circular economic policies and practices within some of the world's largest economies. In addition to policy-making bodies, influential international and non-governmental organisations collaborate with stakeholders from the private sector, academia and civil society to drive the adoption of circular economy practices.

The European Union's policy framework and legislation promoting a circular economy

The European Union has made the transition to a circular and net zero economy one of its policy priorities. By prioritising the transition to circularity, it is determined to achieve its ambitious goal of becoming the first climate-neutral continent by 2050, a commitment embedded in the European Green Deal (European Commission, 2019[2]), the European Union's blueprint for sustainable growth.

Building on the foundation of its initial Circular Economy Package, which included the EU Circular Economy Action Plan in 2015, the European Union further reinforced its commitment in 2020 with a new Circular Economy Action Plan. This plan is one of the main building blocks of the EU Green Agenda, supporting climate neutrality by decoupling economic growth from resource consumption, strengthening EU competitiveness, and facilitating a just and inclusive transition. It outlines a series of ambitious targets, including a commitment to recycling 65% of municipal waste and 75% of packaging waste by 2035, to be attained through measures like reducing single-use plastics and bolstering eco-design principles for extended life cycles.

The European Union's legal framework for the circular economy is intrinsically connected to the "Fit for 55" package, a comprehensive set of legislations aimed at aligning EU policies with the climate goals outlined in the EU Climate Law.

A number of established regulations support the circular economy and further revisions are implemented as proposed in the Circular Economy Action Plan. The following legal instruments collectively create a robust foundation for the transition to a circular economy within the European Union, contributing to resource efficiency and environmental sustainability on a significant scale.

- The Waste Framework Directive defines the core principles of waste management, including waste prevention and recycling targets. The latest proposal for a targeted revision of the directive was published in July 2023 (European Commission, 2023[3]). It aims to introduce a mandatory and harmonised extended producer responsibility scheme for textiles, in line with the EU Strategy for Sustainable and Circular Textiles (European Commission, 2022[4]).
- The Packaging and Packaging Waste Directive sets specific targets for packaging recycling and recovery. It is undergoing revisions to strengthen packaging requirements, with a focus on enhancing packaging reusability and recyclability, promoting the use of recycled materials, and ensuring effective enforcement (European Parliament, 2023[5]). A complementary policy framework for biobased, biodegradable and compostable plastics was also developed (European Commission, 2022[6]).
- In 2022, proposals were adopted for a new Ecodesign for Sustainable Products Regulation (European Commission, 2022[7]), a revised Construction Products Regulation (European Commission, 2022[8]) and the Empowering Consumers for the Green Transition Regulation (European Commission, 2022[9]).

Beyond regulatory and policy mechanisms, the European Union encourages and supports stakeholder involvement in the circular economy transition. The EU Circular Economy Stakeholder Platform, established in 2017, and the Global Alliance on Circular Economy and Resource Efficiency, launched in 2021, represent important forums for collaboration, knowledge exchange and policy development that advance the circular economy on both regional and global scales.

Momentum for the circular economy in the Western Balkans and Albania

Over the years, there has been a constant increase in waste generated per capita in the Western Balkans, with the recycling rate of municipal waste among the economies being very low, whereas resource intensity as a measure of efficiency of resource use has remained comparatively high (OECD, 2021[10]). This situation poses a significant burden on the environment, leading to its degradation, biodiversity loss as well as to water, air and soil pollution, thus contributing to climate change. In addition, the COVID-19 pandemic showed that dependency on globalised linear supply chains and cheap virgin raw materials pose high economic risks, leading to production disruptions and revenue losses, rendering the current linear economic model unsustainable. Against this backdrop, the circular economy has gained prominence as a solution to address critical environmental concerns while fostering sustainable and more resilient economic development.

The Western Balkan leaders expressed their commitment to align with European climate targets of becoming carbon-neutral by 2050 when they signed the Sofia Declaration on the Green Agenda for the Western Balkans on 10 November 2020. As a key component of this agenda, the transition to a circular economy is supported by the European Commission's Regional Economic and Investment Plan. The Green Agenda for the Western Balkans emphasises the need to link regional economic growth and new business opportunities to more sustainable production and consumption practices. This includes encouraging waste prevention, reuse and recycling as well as reducing waste production, increasing resource productivity and reducing pollution, particularly of plastic.

Spurred by a combination of environmental concerns, economic considerations, and regional and EU integration efforts, the adoption of circular economy principles and practices is gaining traction in the Western Balkans. Serbia and Montenegro adopted circular economy roadmaps in 2020 and 2022, respectively, followed by related programmes or strategies and action plans. Kosovo* published its circular

* This designation is without prejudice to positions on status and is in line with United Nations Security Council Resolution 1244/1999 and the Advisory Opinion of the International Court of Justice on Kosovo's declaration of independence.

economy roadmap in March 2023, while Bosnia and Herzegovina is currently preparing such a document. Supported by the OECD, work on circular economy roadmaps in Albania and North Macedonia started at the end of 2022, with the aim of completing them in early 2024. This document represents the results of the efforts undertaken in Albania.

With the active development of its circular economy framework, Albania can address critical aspects of its circular economy. Foremost among these is the challenge of ineffective waste management, a shared concern among regional peers, potentially also impacting Albania's growth as an emerging tourist destination, with the surge in tourism contributing to higher waste quantities and adding to this challenge. Moreover, very little widespread knowledge of the circular concept and opportunities in the broader society and within the business community pose a risk of missing out on vital opportunities for essential and green development investments.

References

Env.net (2021), *Circular Economy Regional Report*, http://env-net.org/wp-content/uploads/2021/01/Circular-Economy-2020.pdf. [11]

European Commission (2023), *Proposal for a Targeted Revision of the Waste Framework Directive*, European Commission, Brussels, https://environment.ec.europa.eu/publications/proposal-targeted-revision-waste-framework-directive_en. [3]

European Commission (2022), "Circular economy: Commission proposes new consumer rights and a ban on greenwashing", press release, https://ec.europa.eu/commission/presscorner/detail/en/ip_22_2098. [9]

European Commission (2022), *Communication – EU Policy Framework on Biobased, Biodegradable and Compostable Plastics*, European Commission, Brussels, https://environment.ec.europa.eu/publications/communication-eu-policy-framework-biobased-biodegradable-and-compostable-plastics_en. [6]

European Commission (2022), *Communication – EU Strategy for Sustainable and Circular Textiles*, European Commission, Brussels, https://environment.ec.europa.eu/publications/textiles-strategy_en. [4]

European Commission (2022), *Proposal for a Regulation Laying Down Harmonised Conditions for the Marketing of Construction Products, Amending Regulation (EU) 2019/1020 and Repealing Regulation (EU) 305/2011*, European Commission, Brussels, https://ec.europa.eu/docsroom/documents/49315. [8]

European Commission (2022), *Proposal for Ecodesign for Sustainable Products Regulation*, European Commission, Brussels, https://environment.ec.europa.eu/publications/proposal-ecodesign-sustainable-products-regulation_en. [7]

European Commission (2019), *Communication on the European Green Deal*, European Commission, Brussels, https://commission.europa.eu/document/daef3e5c-a456-4fbb-a067-8f1cbe8d9c78_en. [2]

European Parliament (2023), *Revision of the Packaging and Packaging Waste Directive*, European Parliament, https://www.europarl.europa.eu/RegData/etudes/BRIE/2023/745707/EPRS_BRI(2023)745707_EN.pdf. [5]

McCarthy, A., R. Dellink and R. Bibas (2018), "The Macroeconomics of the Circular Economy Transition: A Critical Review of Modelling Approaches", *OECD Environment Working Papers*, No. 130, OECD Publishing, Paris, https://doi.org/10.1787/af983f9a-en. [1]

OECD (2021), *Competitiveness in South East Europe 2021: A Policy Outlook*, Competitiveness and Private Sector Development, OECD Publishing, Paris, https://doi.org/10.1787/dcbc2ea9-en. [10]

Note

[1] According to a study conducted in 2020, while more than half of SMEs interviewed declared being familiar with the concept of a circular economy, only 44% had a clear understanding of what a circular economy entails (Env.net, 2021[11]).

2 State-of-play of the circular economy in Albania

This chapter analyses Albania's current circular economy policy landscape and initiatives, focusing on key economic features and environmental implications stemming from energy production, emissions, material use and waste management. By pinpointing gaps in both policy and practice and integrating additional analyses, the chapter provides valuable insights for prioritising areas in future circular economy policy documents to drive Albania's transition to a circular and carbon-neutral economy.

Albania's key economic features and their relevance to the circular economy

Albania has made significant economic progress over the past three decades, moving from a low-income economy to an upper middle-income European Union (EU) candidate state, with gross domestic product (GDP) per capita PPP (constant 2017 international $) rising from 3 265 in 1992 to 15 492 in 2022 (World Bank, 2024[1]). In 2021, 1.25 million people were employed in Albania (44.8% women and 55.2% men), representing 60.9% of the labour force, on an increasing trend since 2014. Albania's economy has grown at moderate rates for most of the last decade, averaging 2.7% between 2012 and 2022 (World Bank, 2023[2]). Since 2020, economic growth has been impacted by external shocks, the first of which was the COVID pandemic. The subsequent energy crisis and inflation, induced by the war in Ukraine, have dampened its economic recovery (Box 2.1).

The breakdown of value added by economic activity shows that the economy is particularly reliant on agriculture, forestry and fishing, followed by trade, transport, and accommodation and food services, largely due to its sizable tourism sector (Figure 2.2).

Box 2.1. Impact of recent crises on Albania's economic growth

- The earthquake that hit Albania in 2019 coupled with the start of the COVID-19 pandemic in 2020 had a strong impact on Albania's gross domestic product (GDP) (Figure 2.1).
- Fast and determined responses from the government and the central bank managed to soften the negative impacts of the pandemic and helped maintain the macroeconomic and financial sector stability.
- Albania rebounded with an 8.9% GDP growth in 2021, thanks to increases in both domestic and foreign demand.
- Nevertheless, inflation rose to an annual average of 7% in 2022, induced by the Russian Federation's ongoing war in Ukraine, leading to the central bank normalising its very loose monetary policy. The economic recovery decelerated but GDP growth was still robust at an estimated 4.8% in 2022, driven by private investment and consumption.

Figure 2.1. GDP growth and inflation in Albania, 2017-2022

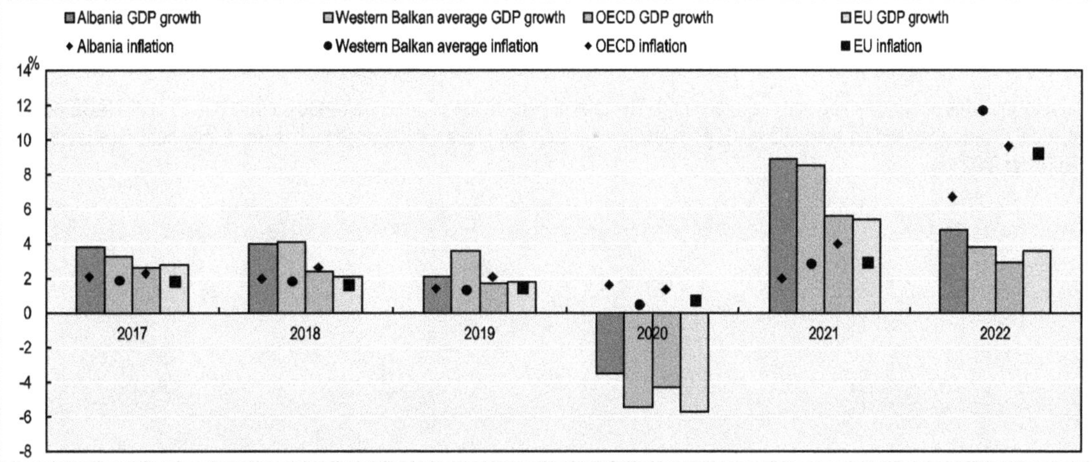

Notes: GDP: gross domestic product; EU: European Union. Data are unavailable for Bosnia and Herzegovina in 2022.
Sources: European Commission (2022[3]); OECD (2023[4]; 2023[5]).

StatLink https://stat.link/z2d31q

Figure 2.2. Value added by economic activity in Albania, 2022

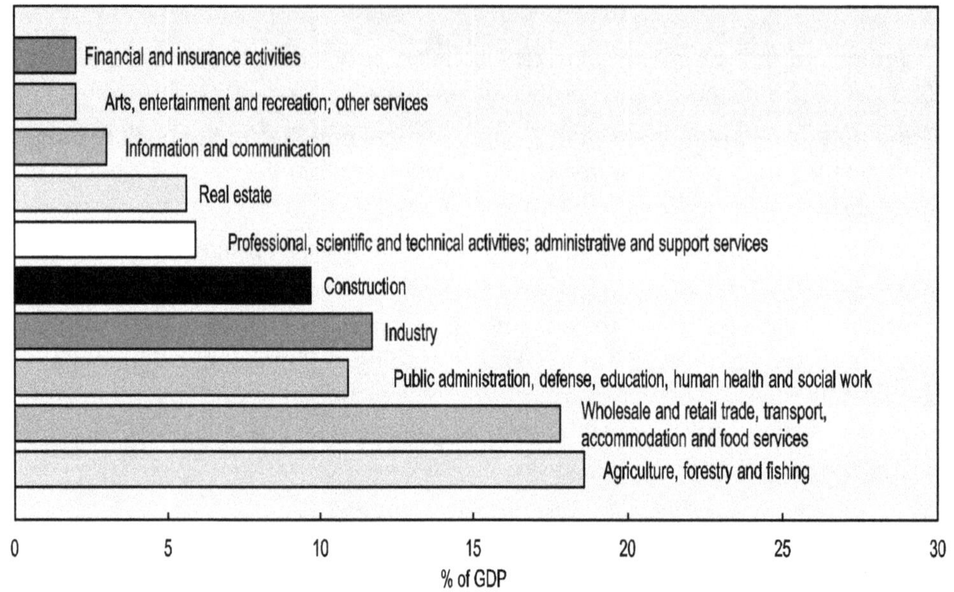

Notes: Industry includes energy, mining and manufacturing. The total of percentage of gross domestic product (GDP) of all NACE activities does not equal 100%. Data are based on estimations. GDP measurement includes gross value added plus taxes, minus subsidies on products.
Source: Eurostat (2023[6]).

Service sector

Services represented 47.2% of GDP and 44% of employment in 2022 (Figure 2.3), holding the highest sectoral share in the GDP and employment of Albania.

Figure 2.3. Value added by grouped activity, 2022, and employment by economic activity in Albania, 2012-2022

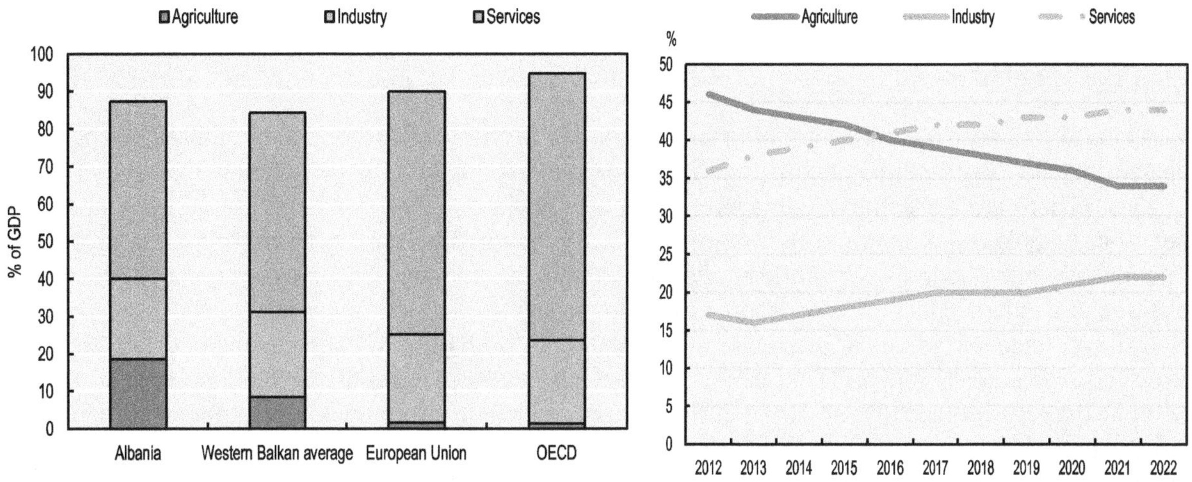

Notes: Industry includes construction, energy, mining and manufacturing. The value-added shares presented in the World Development Indicators for agriculture, industry and services may not add up to 100% due to financial intermediary services indirectly measured and net indirect taxes. 2022 data are based on estimations for some of the Western Balkan economies. Full OECD country data are only available until 2021.

Sources: Eurostat (2023[6]); World Bank (2022[7]); OECD (2024[8]); INSTAT (2023[9]).

StatLink https://stat.link/ynwd8z

Tourism

With tourism representing 17.4% of GDP and 20% of employment in 2021, Albania is highly dependent on tourism exports (AIDA, 2022[10]). Average annual tourist arrivals increased by 13% between 2009 and 2019, and arrivals in the first 10 months of 2022 grew by approximately 17% compared to 2019 – ranking Albania as the highest performing destination in Europe and second in the world,[1] with this increase continuing in 2023 (UNWTO, 2023[11]; EIU, 2022[12]). Nevertheless, the sector's growth is undermined by high seasonality, concentration in coastal areas, poor infrastructure and the lack of a qualified workforce. The value added per tourist is still relatively low because Albania tends to mostly attract short-stay tourists with low spending power, due to the undiversified tourism value chain and a limited range of offered activities (OECD, 2021[13]). On a per-arrival basis, international tourism receipts in Albania are lower than close-by and neighbouring destinations, such as Croatia and Greece (UNWTO, n.d.[14]), and far below the EU average (tourists spent an average of EUR 51 per night in Albania (UNDP, 2022[15]) compared to EUR 87 in the European Union in 2022 (Eurostat, 2023[16])). Moreover, the recent increase in tourism and related investments have caused environmental pressures on coastal areas (OECD, 2021[13]). While tourism has been severely impacted by recent economic shocks, recovery offers unique opportunities to redesign the sector in a sustainable and resilient way in line with a circular economy model, intentionally regenerative of natural, human and social capital, operating within the local destinations' sustainable boundaries (Einarsson and Sorin, 2020[17]).

Industry sector

The industrial sector, including construction and covering energy, mining and manufacturing, remains important for the Albanian economy, representing around one-fifth of GDP (21.4% in 2022), albeit a 5 percentage point decrease over the last ten years. It also accounts for 22% of employment (Figure 2.3). While industry is the most resource-intensive and waste-producing economic sector, it shows tremendous potential for innovation, as the markets for new clean products and services keep growing. Nevertheless, upgrading and diversifying the industry sector in Albania is hindered by low levels of innovation and technology adoption, and thus not boosted by local technical know-how (OECD, 2021[13]).

Textile and footwear

Textile and footwear is an industry of great importance to the Albanian economy, representing 32% of value added in manufacturing in 2021 and 27.8% of total exports in 2022 (World Bank, 2021[18]; INSTAT, 2023[19]). There are more than 1 000 active companies working in the textile and footwear manufacturing sector in Albania, employing mainly women (95%), represented by the Proeksport Albania Association. The industry has a long history in the economy and until the transformations of the early 1990s, used to oversee the entire chain of production, from the production of raw materials to the final products. Nowadays, factories no longer produce raw materials but clothing with imported material, which is then exported. While textile and footwear companies are still mostly responsible for the time-intensive cutting and packaging of products (a so-called cut-make-trim model), in recent years, manufacturing companies have improved their processes and invested in new machinery to offer a full-package service for foreign customers, including the capacity to design products (Invest in Albania, n.d.[20]; ILO and UNIDO, 2023[21]). Digitalisation of the sector is also underway. Projects funded by international development co-operation partners financially and technically support the integration of computer-aided design and computer-aided manufacture tools in design and manufacturing processes.[2]

Nevertheless, production processes for textiles and footwear remain characterised by low recycling, low reuse and underutilisation of fabric, leading to considerable amounts of generated waste. The textile industry is considered to be one of the most polluting and waste-generating sectors globally, contributing to 10% of total carbon emissions worldwide, surpassing aviation and marine shipping (European Commission, 2020[22]). Furthermore, it accounts for 20% of global freshwater pollution and is associated with high rates of landfilling and burning. Its associated carbon dioxide (CO_2) emissions are projected to increase by more than 60% by 2030; "a new textile economy" based on a circular model will, therefore, be key in reaching climate-neutral targets (Design4Circle, 2021[23]). Because Albania's textile companies are not involved in raw material production of fabrics or end-of-life management of clothes or footwear, the circular potential lies in sustainable production processes (manufacturing, treating and dyeing) and waste reduction in cutting and packaging techniques. Moreover, as more and more local enterprises are abandoning the cut-make-trim model and moving towards the full production cycle, moving to a sustainable design of garments could be a key element to restructuring the sector and supporting the transition to a circular model, as around 80% of a product's environmental impact is locked in at the design stage (Design4Circle, 2021[23]; ILO and UNIDO, 2023[21]). Additionally, textile co-labels, for which guidelines have been developed in Albania, could increase demand for green and circular business practices, while also being useful for small and medium-sized enterprises (SMEs) when dealing with business licensing and administrative requirements (OECD, 2021[24]).

Construction

The construction sector's value added has increased in the past decade, accounting for 9.7% of GDP in 2022 (see Figure 2.2). The growth of the sector in recent years was spurred by significant infrastructure and residential development, such as the Reconstruction Programme[3] initiated after the earthquake in 2019, increasing investments in real estate from non-residents and in the tourism sector, as well as major infrastructure projects, including the Trans-Adriatic Pipeline.[4] Additionally, there proves to be long-term growth potential in the construction of renewable energy infrastructure and improvements to transmission lines and the distribution grid.[5] The increased value added of the sector was one of the main contributors to the rapid economic recovery from the COVID-19 pandemic. The sector is expected to further expand, evidenced by the increasing number of construction permits issued in recent years[6] (INSTAT, 2023[25]).

Construction materials and metals is construction's leading sub-sector, representing 21.6% of total exports in Albania in 2022, with aluminium, iron, steel and cement being the most exported products (INSTAT, 2023[19]; World Bank, 2023[26]). Albania's main export destinations are EU countries, with the majority of products exported to Italy.

These industries are, nevertheless, energy- and carbon-intensive, lack modern technology, and the production of secondary materials from material waste is almost non-existent (Ministry of Infrastructure and Energy, 2016[27]). Overall, untapped potential remains in the production of sustainable construction materials, in particular through more resource-efficient mining operations and the use of industrial waste and reuse of construction materials. Moreover, transitioning to circular production processes of construction products might be beneficial in light of the EU Carbon Border Adjustment Mechanism.[7]

Mining and quarrying

Mining and quarrying accounted for 2.2% of GDP in 2021 (INSTAT, 2023[28]) and for 11.4% of total exports in 2022 (INSTAT, 2023[29]) and has a long-standing history in the economy (National Agency of Natural Resources, 2022[30]). Albania is rich in different mineral resources. Those mined and treated in its territory include mainly chrome, copper, iron-nickel and coal. As of February 2023, there were 554 active mining permits (Ministry of Infrastructure and Energy, 2023[31]) and over 100 business entities involved in mining and quarrying activities, employing 0.46% of the workforce (excluding processing), 64% of it in the chromium subsector (Extractive Industries Transparency Initiative, 2020[32]).

In 1994, the Law on Mining opened the mining sector up to private investments. Processing levels in Albania, however, remain relatively low, and metal ores are mainly exported as raw material with low added value for further processing in the destination countries (National Agency of Natural Resources, 2022[33]). To tackle these issues, the sector is increasingly seeking to attract strategic and substantial investments in the processing of metal ores. In addition, the government recently introduced a tax exemption for domestically processed minerals to redirect investment into processing and counter unsustainable material consumption in the mining sector (Gjonaj, 2020[34]). Yet, insufficient clean-up and remediation of mining sites remain evident. Coupled with unsustainable extraction methods, mining activities pose a potentially serious risk to environmental and human health through the release of hazardous chemicals and air, water and soil pollution and contamination (UNECE, 2018[35]). Enhancing circularity during the mining operations stage and recovering essential raw materials from extractive waste in ongoing mining operations and historical mining waste sites could ensure the sustainability of critical raw materials and safeguard the environment from hazardous and toxic elements.

Agriculture

Agriculture's value added in Albania has been stagnating at around 20% over the past decade (18.6% of GDP in 2022) and is still the highest in the Western Balkans (where it stood at 9% on average in 2022) and remains well above the EU and OECD averages (1.7% and 1.4%, respectively, in 2022) (Figure 2.3) (OECD, 2021[13]). Despite a decline of 12 percentage points in the last decade, agriculture still represented 34% of employment in 2022 (Figure 2.3), with most jobs being low-skilled and low-wage, mainly due to the prevalence of subsistence farming (Ministry of Agriculture and Rural Development, 2022[36]; Invest in Albania, 2023[37]).

A share of 40.5% of Albanian land is used for agriculture, but the sector is dominated by a large number of very small and fragmented farms (the average farm size is around 1.2 hectares, or one-tenth the size of the EU27 average) (European Commission, 2023[38]; World Bank, 2023[26]). This has a significant impact on the sector's competitiveness and productivity, which is among the lowest in Europe (Ministry of Agriculture and Rural Development, 2022[36]). In addition to land fragmentation, inadequate irrigation (only 19.6% of land was irrigated and only 57% of the rural population had access to water services in 2021) and transport infrastructure, as well as limited access to finance, hinder the development of a competitive, export-oriented agriculture and agribusiness sector (World Bank, 2022[39]). Agricultural exports, while increasing, remain relatively low and are dominated by the fruit and vegetable sector (which represents more than one-third of agriculture exports) (Ministry of Tourism and Environment, 2019[40]; OECD, 2021[13]). The European Union remains Albania's most important partner for both the export and import of agri-food commodities (63% of total agri-food exports and 62% of imports during 2022), whereas the Western Balkan region is destination to 26.4% of the agri-food exports and origin of 12.3% of agri-food imports (INSTAT, 2023[41]). In 2022, agri-food exports from Albania to the Western Balkans and the European Union reached a record high of EUR 473 million, an 18.5 % increase compared to the previous year (Ministry of Agriculture and Rural Development, 2023[42]).

Despite favorable climatic conditions and ongoing efforts to standardise regulations, a high percentage of agricultural farms in Albania do not meet national and EU standards. This is mainly due to limited financial resources for facility and technology improvements and a lack of knowledge about these standards. However, there are vast opportunities to enhance the competitiveness of Albania's agricultural products in regional markets (Ministry of Agriculture and Rural Development, 2022[36]). The main agricultural products produced in Albania in 2022 were vegetables (1.3 million tonnes), followed by cereals (0.69 million tonnes). Vegetable production in greenhouses represented 22.9% of total vegetable production in 2022, where tomato production represents 51.6% of total production (INSTAT, 2023[43]). Moreover, olive cultivation has increased over the last 15 years (157 000 tonnes in 2022, up by 43% from 2021), in part due to heavy state subsidies, which made Albania the leading olive oil producer in the Western Balkans, though its current production still represents only 0.6% of total EU production (INSTAT, 2023[43]; OECD, 2021[13]). Despite having taken steps, there is a need to improve olive farming technology; support technology renovation for a significant part of processing plants; increase investments in olive oil storing, bottling, labelling and packaging capacity; and ensure olive waste treatment according to the standards (Ministry of Agriculture and Rural Development, 2022[36]). About half of farmers are engaged in livestock production (mainly cattle, sheep and goats), and while dairy output has increased significantly, there is considerable scope to expand dairy exports further (World Bank, 2022[39]; INSTAT, 2023[43]).

A circular transition could foster growth in the sector by ensuring sustainable agricultural production, an increase of the use of food surplus, technological progress and an efficient use of resources in order to prevent further depletion and over-exploitation of natural resources (OECD, 2019[44]). By adopting circular economy principles, the sector could improve water, energy and waste management while protecting biodiversity and enabling the sustainable development of local communities, thus contributing to other sectors' goals, such as tourism.

SME sector

SMEs constituted 99.8% of all enterprises and 81.6% of employment in 2021, slightly higher shares than in the European Union (98.9% of all enterprises and 67% of employment) (INSTAT, 2023[45]; OECD, 2022[46]; Eurostat, 2020[47]). Services represent the main economic activities for more than 85% of SMEs in Albania, with the largest share of SMEs working in the trade sector (39.2%), followed by accommodation and restaurants (16.4%), mainly due to the growing importance of the tourism sector. Moreover, around 13% of SMEs work in the industry sector (mainly construction, manufacturing, and mining and quarrying)[8] (INSTAT, 2023[45]).

While climate change mitigation policies have historically focused on large emitters, SMEs, on aggregate, have a significant environmental footprint (small firms account for 50% of greenhouse [GHG] emissions in the world (ICT, 2021[48]) and 63% in the European Union (European Commission, 2022[49])). It is, hence, essential that Albania considers them in its environmental policy making. On the one hand, SMEs, like any other economic agent, face the effects of environmental degradation, which can pose specific challenges for their survival and growth. On the other hand, and more importantly, the large share of SMEs in Albania can be a source of innovation and solutions to develop the technologies needed to address environmental challenges and achieve circular objectives, both due to SMEs' flexibility in adopting circular business models ("green performers") and their contribution in developing new products, technologies and approaches that address environmental issues ("green innovators") (OECD, 2021[50]). However, only 20% of Albanian businesses believe that their business models allow for a shift towards a circular economy, with added costs and the lack of government subsidies being the most significant impediments in this regard (RCC, 2023[51]).

Environmental trends and recent developments relevant to the circular economy

Energy use and emissions trends

As a Non-Annex-I signatory to the United Nations Framework Convention on Climate Change and its Paris Agreement and a party to the Kyoto Protocol, Albania has committed to an 11.5% reduction of CO_2 emissions compared to the baseline for the period 2016-30, based on a business-as-usual scenario. Moreover, in line with the European Union's ambition to become climate-neutral by 2050, Albania has also committed to achieving carbon neutrality by 2050 by endorsing the Green Agenda for the Western Balkans.

CO_2 emissions account for around two-thirds of Albania's total GHG emissions. An inventory of other pollutants (SO_2, CH_4, N_2O, hydrofluorocarbons) is available as part of Albania's Fourth Communication to the United Nations Framework Convention on Climate Change for the period 2009-19 (including emissions estimates from energy; industrial processes and product use; agriculture; land use, land-use change and forestry; and waste) (Ministry of Tourism and Environment, 2022[52]).

In 2022, Albania had the lowest GHG emissions per capita (2.71 tonnes of CO_2 equivalent per capita) in the Western Balkan region and compared to the EU and OECD averages (8.1 and 9.9 tonnes CO_2 equivalent per capita, respectively) (Crippa et al., 2023[53]). However, when looking at the trend over the past two decades, while the OECD and European Union have made significant progress in reducing their emissions per capita, they almost tripled up to 2017 (3.17 tonnes of CO_2 equivalent per capita) in Albania, but have since been slowly decreasing (JRC/IEA, 2023[54]; Eurostat, 2023[55]). Likewise, a different picture emerges when considering the carbon intensity of national income. Although significantly lower than its regional peers, Albania produced approximately 0.175 tonnes of CO_2 equivalent/1 000 USD/GDP per 2017 PPP, placing it at a similar level to the European Union (0.186 tonnes of CO_2 equivalent/1 000 USD/GDP) in 2022 (JRC/IEA, 2023[54]). Oil and oil products are the largest source of CO_2 emissions in Albania, representing 70% of total emissions (Figure 2.4). Transport, and in particular road transport, is the sector with the greatest oil demand and the one that emits the most CO_2 in Albania, accounting for over a third of total emissions (35% in 2022) (JRC/IEA, 2023[54]). Albania is the exception in the region and compared to the European Union in this regard, where transport only accounts for 20.5% and 27.5% of total emissions on average, respectively.

Figure 2.4. CO_2 emissions by source in Albania, 2021

% of total CO_2 emissions

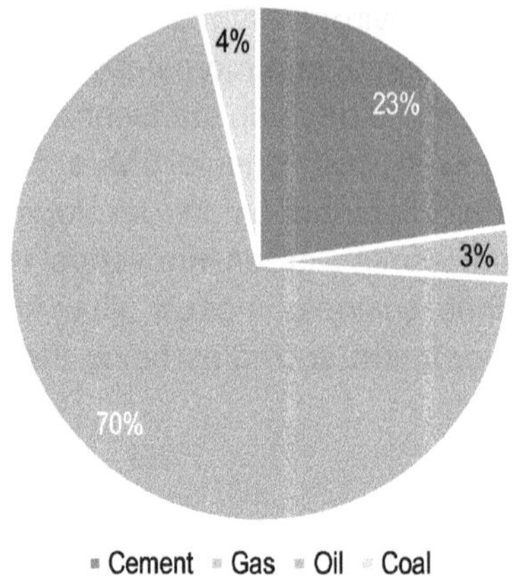

Source: Ritchie, Roser and Rosado (2022[56]).

While Western Balkan economies are, on average, over-reliant on coal (Figure 2.5), it accounts for a much smaller share in Albania (10%) and contributes to a minor share of total CO_2 emissions, due to higher reliance on oil and renewables (Figure 2.4). Natural gas also plays a smaller role for the primary energy consumption mix (2%) than in the European Union (23%). This share is expected to increase as Albania recently connected to an international natural gas pipeline via the Trans-Adriatic Pipeline (OECD, 2021[13]).

Figure 2.5. Energy mix in Albania, the Western Balkans and the European Union, 2021

% of total energy

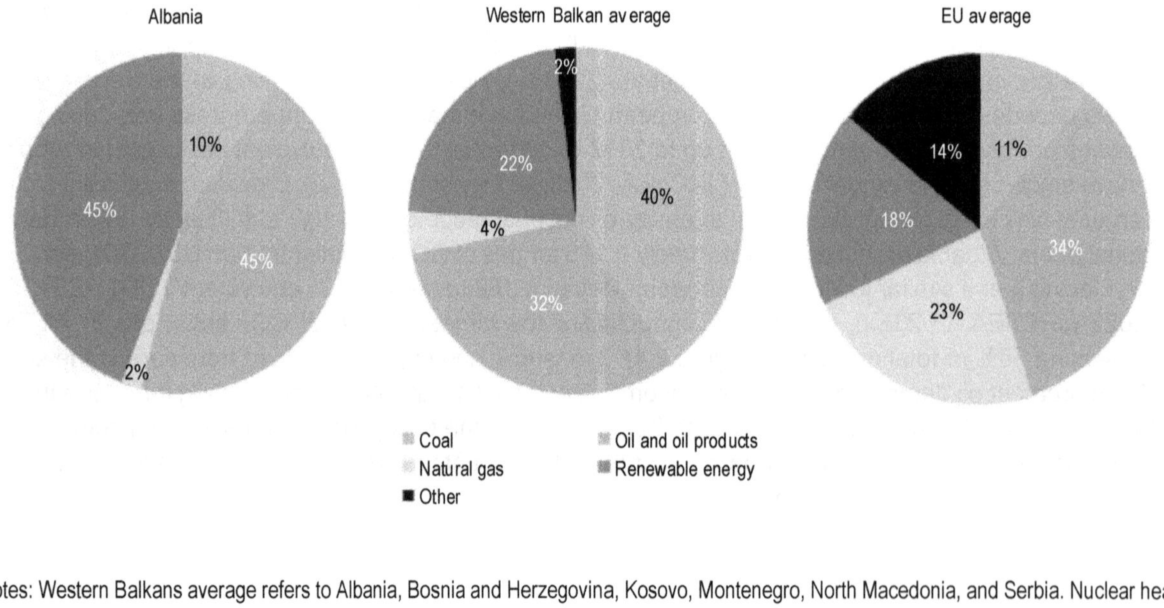

Notes: Western Balkans average refers to Albania, Bosnia and Herzegovina, Kosovo, Montenegro, North Macedonia, and Serbia. Nuclear heat accounts for 12.8% of the European Union's energy mix. The major types of renewable energy sources are biomass (wood and wood waste, municipal solid waste, landfill gas and biogas, biofuels), hydropower, geothermal, wind and solar. Totals may not add up to a 100% due to net imported or exported electricity.
Source: Eurostat (2023[57]).

With Albania being one of the few economies in the region producing crude oil, almost half of its energy supply is covered by oil and oil products – the highest share in the Western Balkans. However, the crude oil that is produced is mostly exported to be refined abroad (Altax, 2019[58]).

Renewable energy accounts for a significant share of Albania's energy mix – approximately 45%, a higher share than its regional peers, 73% of which is derived from hydro generation (Eurostat, 2023[57]). Albania is, however, almost entirely dependent on hydropower for its electricity supply. This gives it an advantage in decarbonising its electricity sector but also makes it highly vulnerable to the changing climate; important annual fluctuations due to hydrological changes mean that Albania has to import electricity most years[9] (Eurostat, 2022[59]). In recent years, Albania has been increasing the share of other renewable energy sources in line with its energy commitments, particularly through renewable energy auctions (solar and wind).[10]

Moreover, Albania had higher energy intensity of GDP than the European Union in 2020 (196 and 117 kilogrammes of oil equivalent per EUR 1 000 respectively), making its industries more vulnerable to rising energy prices. High energy intensity is largely a consequence of both the low-cost electricity supply based on hydro and the slow rollout of investments in energy efficiency (Eurostat, 2023[60]). However, over the past decade, energy intensity in Albania has shown a decreasing trend, steadily converging with levels observed in the European Union.

The long-term sustainability of the energy sector in Albania will be dependent on improving water resource management for continued reliance on hydropower, diversifying the energy mix through other renewable sources and curbing demand growth through energy efficiency measures. Introducing circular economy strategies into hydropower generation could ensure its sustainability, as hydropower plants and dams can create greater value, such as contributing to cleaning rivers with equipped trash racks and cleaning machines or improving water management services with water-tracking devices for better climate forecasts. If environmental protection is ensured for hydro generation investments,[11] designing durable and easily disassembled and recycled hydropower plants (their lifetime can exceed 100 years) can be significant to long-term low-carbon electricity. When it comes to investments in other renewable sources (solar and wind), obtaining the materials they require – in particular lithium, cobalt and rare earths – exclusively via mining presents sustainability and energy security[12] challenges (Pennington, 2022[61]). Renewable material recycling and the use of secondary low-carbon materials will, therefore, be vital to support the clean energy transition.

Materials use

Albania is endowed with considerable natural resources, including water, arable lands (of which 24% is used for agriculture), natural gas reserves, oil (220 million barrels), coal (575 million tonnes of proven coal reserves), metallic mineral deposits (gold, chromium, copper, iron-nickel), rock (travertine, limestone, dolomite), and a wide variety of freshwater and saltwater fish (Environment Go, 2022[62]; National Agency of Natural Resources, 2022[33]).

Domestic material consumption (DMC), or the total amount of materials extracted and used from the environment, taking into account the physical trade balance, stood at 7.2 tonnes per capita in 2021, below the EU and OECD averages, which amounted to 14.1 tonnes per capita (in 2021) and 17.5 tonnes per capita (in 2019), respectively. Albania's DMC is dominated by biomass (wood, food), followed by non-metallic minerals (industrial and construction minerals), which combined account for 82% of the total. Fossil energy materials and carriers and metal ores amounted to 8% each (Figure 2.6).

Biomass' share in Albania's DMC (42%) is much higher than in the European Union, where it only accounts for about a quarter of total DMC (Eurostat, 2022[63]), due to the high contribution of agriculture to Albania's GDP and the use of firewood for various heating applications (IRENA, 2021[64]). The circular transition of biomass and the development of a circular bioeconomy could be significant in meeting climate targets and protecting the environment, through better policies guiding more resource-efficient and sustainable primary production and waste management (composting and anaerobic digestion) and supporting the use of residues and wastes in agricultural practices. Moreover, bio-waste conversion to energy could support Albania's climate targets by reducing its reliance on fossil energy materials.

Additionally, the production of non-metallic minerals, relatively low-value bulk commodities which are essential for Albania's construction sector, is resource- and energy-intensive, due to the several steps necessary for their transformation (such as grinding, heating, mixing, cutting, shaping and honing) (OECD, 2019[65]). Resource efficiency efforts in all non-metallic materials' life cycles will be important to reduce emissions and minimise the environmental impacts.

Figure 2.6. Structure of domestic material consumption in Albania, 2021

% of total

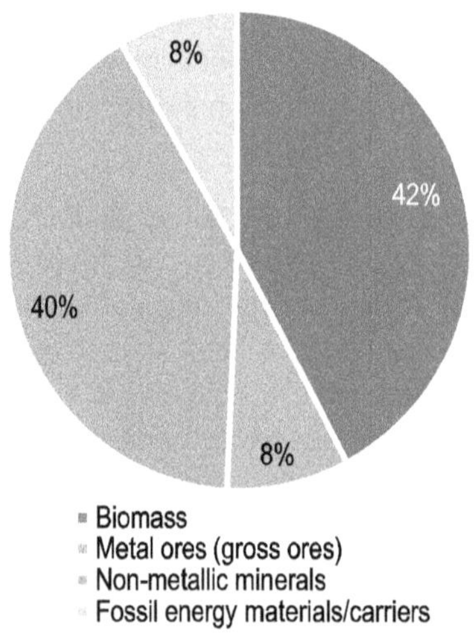

Source: INSTAT (2023[66]).

Between 2017 and 2021, Albania witnessed changes in its DMC. The DMC of non-metallic minerals decreased by approximately 20%, while biomass consumption remained stable. In contrast, there was a noteworthy 22% increase in the consumption of fossil energy materials and nearly a doubling in the consumption of metal ores (INSTAT, 2023[66]). These shifts have led to a slight restructuring of Albania's DMC, with the proportion of metal ores doubling during this period and that of non-metallic minerals decreasing by more than 5 percentage points. In addition to the increasing consumption of fossil energy materials and metal ores, their import dependencies have remained the most significant (Figure 2.7). A transition to a circular economy could positively contribute to decreasing these dependencies, in particular since metal ores can be recycled indefinitely without losing quality or purity, particularly iron, steel and aluminium – metals which are the most extracted in Albania (INSTAT, 2022[67]).

Figure 2.7. Import dependency in Albania, 2010-2021

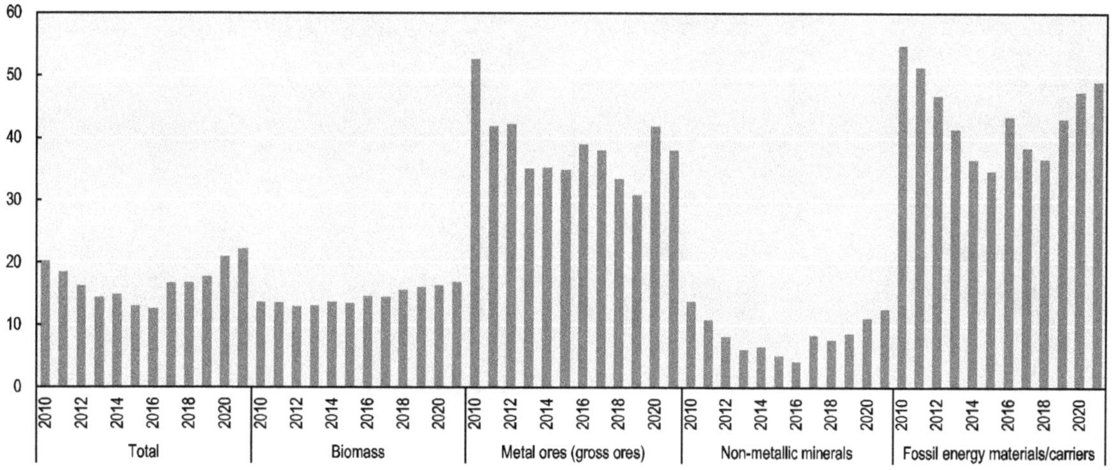

Notes: Import dependency is the ratio of imports over direct material inputs (DMI). DMI is calculated as the sum of domestic extraction of natural resources and imports of materials.
Source: INSTAT (2023[66]).

StatLink https://stat.link/wd37lq

With Albania's DMC per capita on a slight decreasing trend since 2016 (when it was 9.9 tonnes per capita), resource productivity has been on a constant increase, reaching an all-time high in Albania in 2021 at 0.75 EUR/kg, marking a sharp increase starting in 2016 (Figure 2.8). While resource productivity is low and still falls short of the EU average (2.1 EUR/kg), these recent trends can be interpreted as a first sign of relative decoupling of economic growth and consumption of natural resources, which could be further accelerated with the transition to a circular economy. Overall, further efforts are needed to increase resource efficiency and productivity at all stages of the material life cycle (extraction, transport, manufacturing, consumption, recovery and disposal) and throughout supply chains. A transition to a circular economy, through repair, reuse and recycle, would reduce material extraction levels, ensure the sustainable flow of resources and offer possibilities to reduce dependencies (OECD, 2021[68]).

Figure 2.8. Resource productivity, 2012-2021

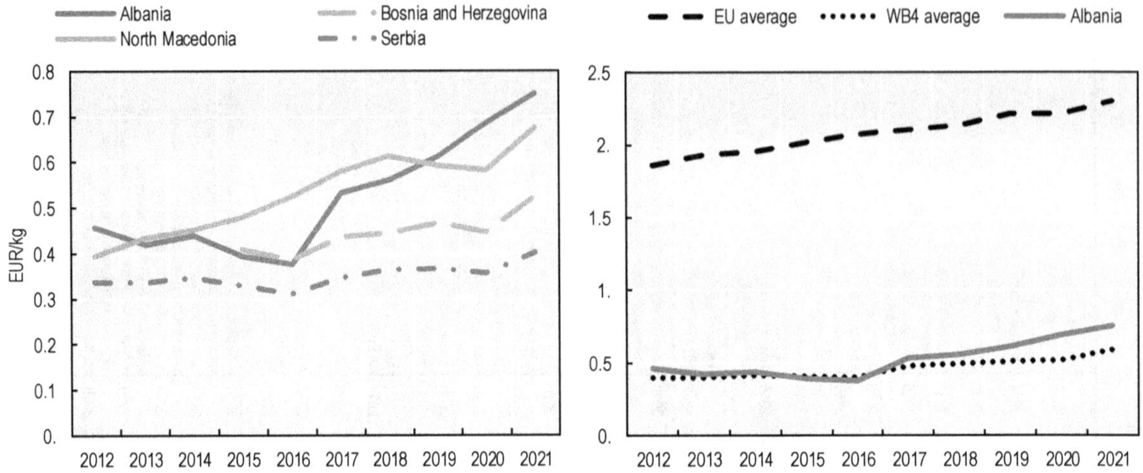

Notes: EU: European Union. WB4: Western Balkans 4: Albania, Bosnia and Herzegovina, North Macedonia, and Serbia; DMC: domestic material consumption. Resource productivity presents the gross domestic product (GDP) divided by DMC. DMC measures the total amount of materials directly used by an economy. No data are available for Bosnia and Herzegovina (before 2014), Kosovo, or Montenegro.
Source: INSTAT (2023[66]); Eurostat (2022[63]; 2022[69]).

Figure 2.9. GDP and domestic material consumption in Albania, 2012-2021

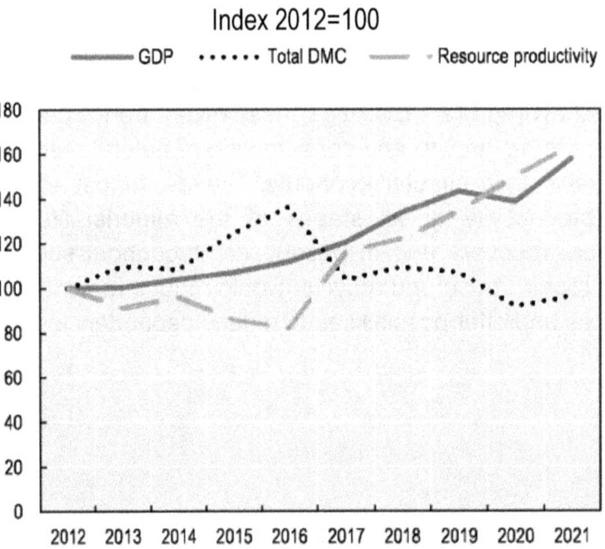

StatLink https://stat.link/4vqfd5

Waste-related trends

Albania's level of municipal waste generation is in the midfield compared to its neighbouring economies, with a slight decreasing trend over recent years (Figure 2.10). Municipal waste dropped from 1.4 million tonnes in 2015 (corresponding to 491 kg/capita) to 0.9 million tonnes in 2021 (corresponding to 311 kg/capita) (Eurostat, 2021[70]). However, this decrease is attributed to the improvement in waste reporting over years[13] and thus cannot point to a reducing trend per se (EEA, 2021[71]). Nevertheless, the data are still not considered of high quality as there are no exact statistics for waste generation; data and reports are instead based on municipalities' and recycling companies' estimations, except for the few municipalities that take their waste to a sanitary landfill or incinerator equipped with weighing devices (EEA, 2021[71]). There are some ongoing efforts to improve waste statistics. Between 2020 and 2022, the Ministry of Tourism and Environment conducted a waste data collection and weighting exercise in all 61 municipalities (National Environmental Agency, 2022[72]) with the aim of increasing awareness of waste quantities and reducing discrepancies between estimated and weighted waste. The waste data obtained through this weighing exercise in Albania for 2022 indicate a notable amount of waste per municipality and a substantial per capita waste generation. However, given that data for all municipalities were only collected for one year and technical structures vary considerably at the local level, they significantly differ from the administrative data. Data are expected to converge more closely in the future if these practices are continued and professionalised.

Figure 2.10. Municipal waste generation, 2013-2021

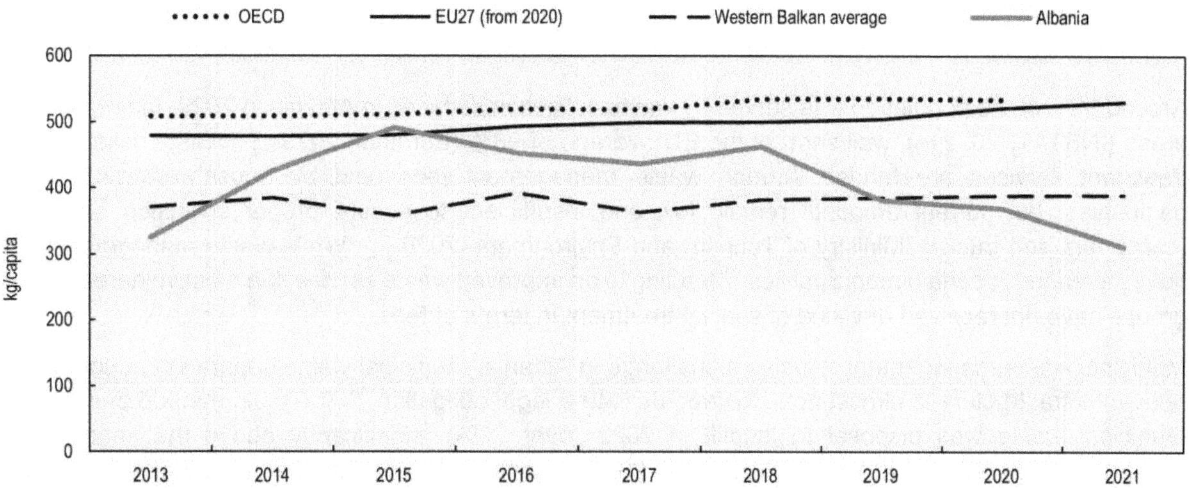

Sources: Eurostat (2021[70]); data for OECD only available until 2020 (OECD, 2022[73]).

StatLink https://stat.link/x19kz4

In 2022, 58.1% of municipal waste produced in Albania was organic,[14] followed by 9.2% of plastic and 8.9% of paper waste (Figure 2.11) (EEA, 2022[74]). When it comes to plastic waste, although Albania is not the largest contributor to plastic pollution in the Adriatic-Ionian basin, its plastic leakage into these natural waters, at 20 kg per person, lies in the higher range among the economies concerned (World Bank, 2020[75]). Another critical point to consider is the fact that a high share of waste, including plastics, is being discharged untreated into the Mediterranean basin from Albania, due to the high proportion of mismanaged waste (73% of total generated waste) (Dalberg Advisors, WWF Mediterranean Marine Initiative, 2019[76]), with litter from fishing and shipping in the Adriatic Sea further adding to the problem of land-based pollution (European Commission, 2020[77]).

Figure 2.11. Waste by compound in Albania, 2013-2022

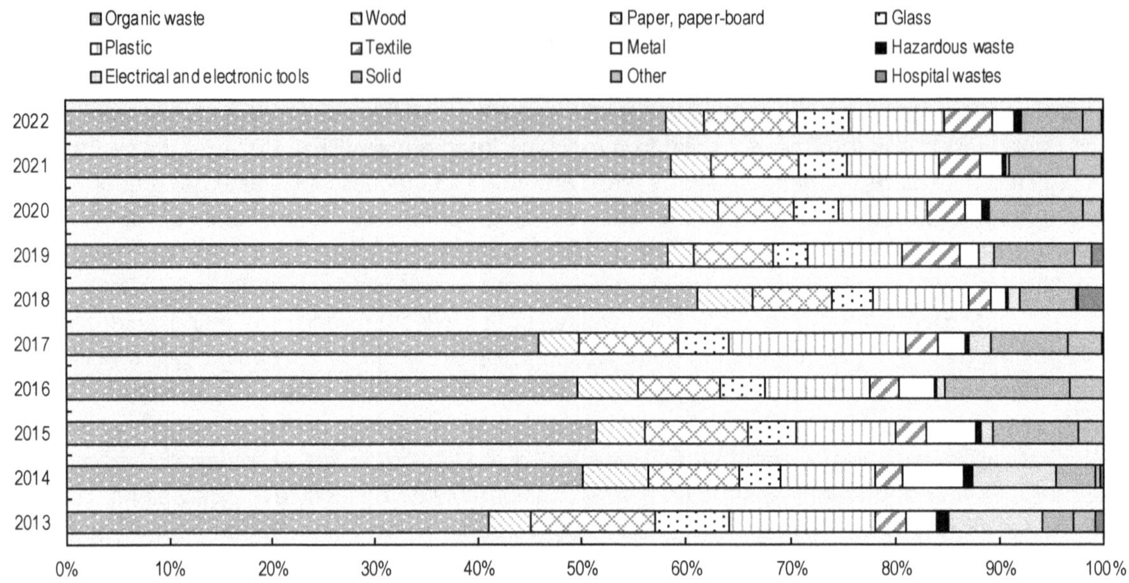

Source: INSTAT (2023[78]).

StatLink https://stat.link/tvz6h1

Around 89% of the population was served by waste collection services in Albania in 2022, mainly in urban areas (INSTAT, 2022[79]), well short of the EU average of 98% (Eurostat, 2023[80]). Waste collection and treatment services are funded through waste management fees paid by households and private companies, but current amounts remain low and insufficient to ensure proper collection equipment (containers and trucks) (Ministry of Tourism and Environment, 2020[81]). While waste management fees have increased in certain municipalities,[15] leading to an improved waste service, the most vulnerable social groups have not received any kind of special treatment in terms of fees.

Municipal waste management remains a challenge in Albania. Municipal waste separation at source and relevant infrastructure is almost non-existent, despite a legal obligation.[16] The main method of managing municipal waste was disposal to landfill in 2022 (over 70%), significantly above the share in the European Union (23%) (Figure 2.12) (Eurostat, 2021[70]). A few pilot projects are, nevertheless, underway to introduce separate collection in some Albanian cities (in particular for paper and cardboard, aluminium, plastics, and bio-waste)[17]. Moreover, the government reported that three composting plants have recently been established (Cerrik, Roskovec and Belsh) and three material recovery facilities (Saranda, Himara and Prrenjas) are operating across Albania, with ten additional plants to be opened in the next four years.

Although higher than in other regional economies, recycling rates of municipal waste in Albania are low (17% in 2022) compared to the EU average (49% in 2021) (Figure 2.12) (Eurostat, 2021[70]). Five recycling plants are operational in the Bushat, Korca and Vlora landfills, and plans are ongoing for the plants to be established at the remaining landfills. While collection for recycling is conducted at sanitary landfills and at the incinerator plant in Elbasan by staff employed to do so, the majority of recyclable waste is still collected by informal waste pickers from dumpsites and bins and sold to the recycling industry[18] (OECD, 2021[13]). The following processes then take place:

- paper and cardboard are sorted in small quantities at the three paper mills (Tirana, Fier and Durres)
- glass bottles are sterilised and reused by beverage companies

- the majority of aluminium cans are exported to neighbouring economies and a small share is directed to a private Albanian smelter
- steel and scrap are sent to the Elbasan metallurgical plant (EEA, 2021[71]).

Figure 2.12. Municipal waste generation and treatment in Albania, 2017-2022

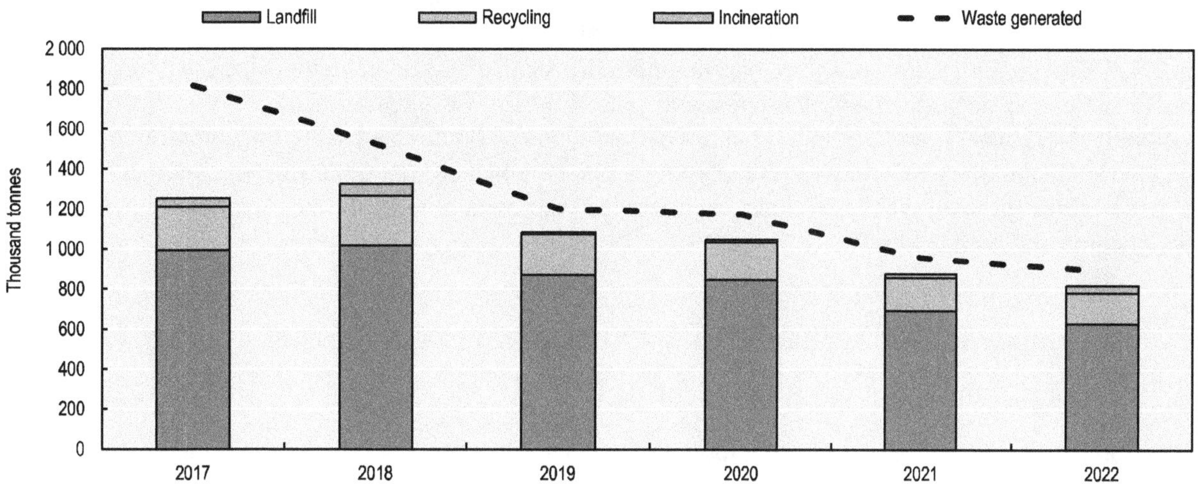

Sources: INSTAT (2023[82]; 2023[83]).

StatLink https://stat.link/nhmqcu

There are more than 30 private recycling companies in Albania (part of the Association of Recyclers of Albania) in charge of these processes. The industry's investment market value is estimated to reach around EUR 230 million. These companies' combined processing capacity is about 500 000 tonnes/year, which is more than enough to process all recyclable waste generated in the economy.[19] Nevertheless, due to the lack of raw material, the companies have reported to be working at around 25% of their production capacity, recycling around 10% of the total municipal waste generated (Ministry of Tourism and Environment, 2020[81]).

Moreover, the first incineration plant in Albania started operating in 2019 in Elbasan, which treated around 2% of municipal waste for energy purposes in 2021 (incineration data prior to 2019 are related to illegal burning of waste at landfills) (EEA, 2021[71]). The construction of two additional waste incinerators in Fier and Tirana, as part of the government's plans to replace the estimated 199 large uncontrolled dumpsites and various small sites still in operation by 2028,[20] have not yet been completed. Nevertheless, recent investments in waste incineration plants should not come at the expense of Albania's recycling industry and should not diverge the country from aligning with the EU *acquis* waste hierarchy principle, recycling targets and a circular model[21] (European Commission, 2022[84]). In addition to the new incinerator plants, a new sanitary landfill is in the planning stage in Vlora and ten illegal landfills are in the process of being approved for remediation to be used while sanitary landfills are constructed (EEA, 2021[71]).

Few data are available on the quantity and management of industrial waste. Key industrial waste generators in Albania include the oil industry, cement production, and steel and mining (EEA, 2018[85]). Mining waste is estimated to amount to more than 45 million tonnes[22] (Thanas, Bode and Mati, 2022[86]) and in 2022, around 12% of total waste managed by municipalities came from industrial production (INSTAT, 2023[78]). Industrial waste is also largely disposed in waste landfills or unmanaged. These sites pose a serious threat to the environment, as industrial waste products have particularly dangerous properties, causing pollution in water, soil and crops.

Treating waste according to the waste hierarchy, through higher recovery and recycling rates of municipal and industrial waste, will be vital to aligning with EU waste legislation, including its recycling and landfill reduction targets. The large amounts of organic waste (see Figure 2.11) generated by municipal and agricultural waste could be further turned into compost and used as a resource for organic soil fertilisers or as a source of biomass to generate biofuels, thus reducing the cost of purchasing new raw materials or products. Mining waste could potentially be used as a commodity and provide solutions to limited metal supplies, such as to backfill mining voids; as a construction material for restoring old mining sites; and as aggregates in embankment, road, pavement, foundation and building construction (EIT Raw Materials, 2021[87]). The cement industry, with its high-temperature kilns, may also have the capacity to utilise certain waste materials, such as used oils, tyres and plastic waste, as alternative sources of energy or raw materials. Moreover, in addition to the ban on certain types of single-use plastic bags introduced in 2022, circular solutions are necessary to further reduce plastic pollution, generated by its untenable use and disposal of (single-use) plastic products, as it comes with several risks for the Albanian tourism sector, ecosystems and human health.

Existing policy landscape and initiatives relevant to the circular economy in Albania

Although no specific policy framework targets the circular economy, the concept is gaining momentum in Albania. Some activities have been undertaken to promote a circular transition in the economy, primarily by international partners, civil society and academia, but they remain rather uncoordinated and *ad hoc*.

Overview of the Albanian circular economy policy landscape

In Albania, the Ministry of Tourism and Environment – in particular the newly established Directorate for Circular Economy – the Ministry of Finance and Economy, the Ministry of Infrastructure and Energy, and the National Agency of Environment are the most relevant institutions for the conception and implementation of circular economy policies. The Albanian Investment Development Agency can also play an important role in promoting circular business models, considering its expanding role as a government business support services provider. Moreover, the Institute of Statistics is instrumental in providing essential data and insights that support informed decision making on the circular economy transition.

The current legal and policy frameworks, including national regulations, strategic documents and action plans, do not provide a solid basis for the circular economy transition. Nevertheless, strategies across a number of thematic areas are considered to be relevant in the circular economy context (Figure 2.13).

Albania lacks an umbrella policy framework on environmental protection, although a comprehensive National Strategy for Climate Change was adopted in 2019, which includes a priority on waste management and reduction. Stemming from Figure 2.13, Table 2.1 outlines policy documents (regional and national) that are relevant to the circular economy, classified into "core" and "directly related". Documents identified as "core" directly reference the circular economy.

Figure 2.13. Overview of the Albanian policy landscape relevant to the circular economy

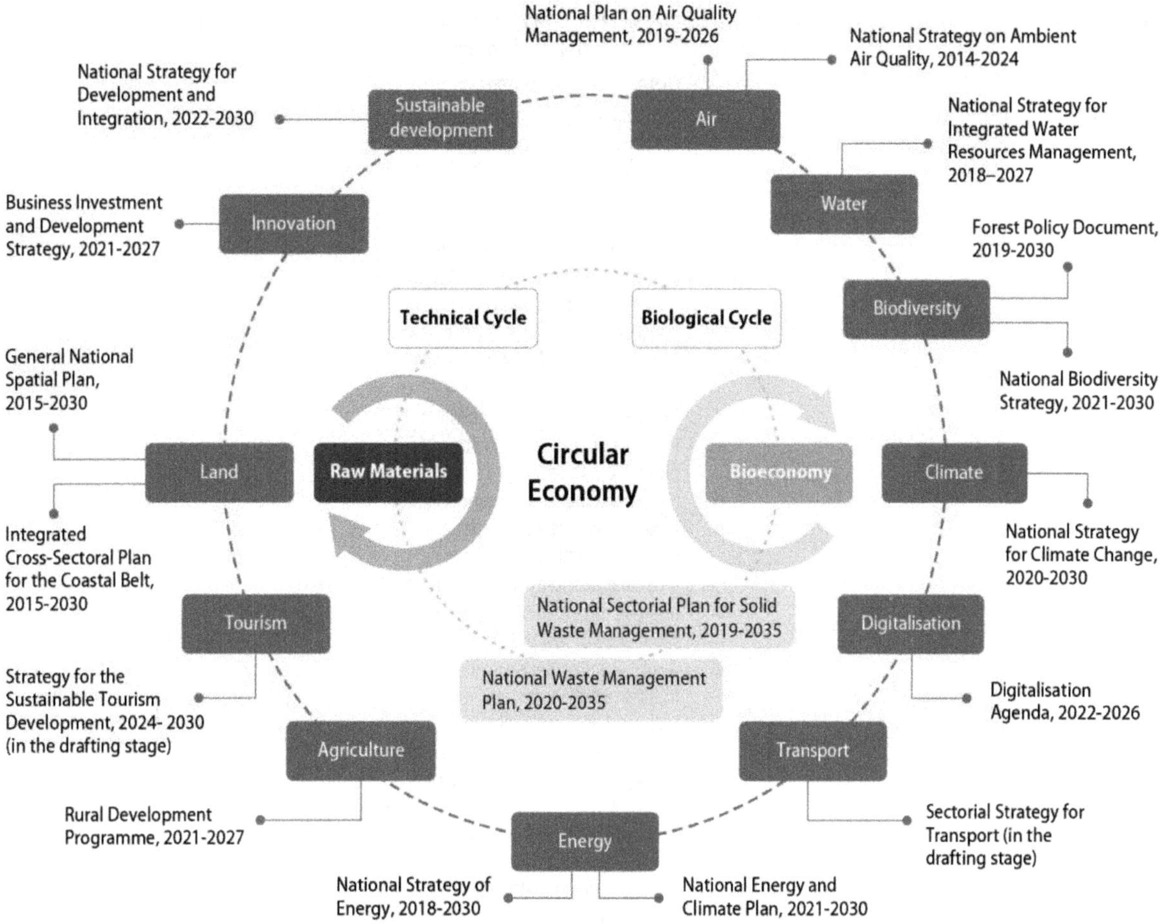

Notes: This policy analysis covered policy documents currently in place and identified across a number of thematic areas considered to be relevant for the transition to a circular economy. This thematic scope includes both technical and biological cycles in the circular economy, as well as policy frameworks enabling this transition. The examples of relevant policies in the circular economy context are not exhaustive.

Table 2.1. List of overarching policy documents relevant to the circular economy in Albania

Topic area	Title	Time frame	Qualitative goals relevant to the circular economy	Quantitative targets
			Core policy documents	
Overarching Green Agenda	Green Agenda for the Western Balkans	2020-30	• Overarching green growth strategy for the Western Balkans, to transition from a traditional economic model to a sustainable economy, in line with the European Green Deal • Alignment of the region with the European Union's (EU) 2050 ambition to make Europe a carbon-neutral continent • Unlock the potential of the circular economy • Fight air, water and soil pollution • Promote sustainable methods of food production and supply • Exploit the region's tourism potential, focusing on protecting biodiversity and ecosystem restoration For the circular economy specifically: • Improve the sustainability of primary production of raw materials • Apply an industrial ecosystem approach to attain environmentally sustainable, balanced economic recovery • Develop circular economy strategies looking at the entire life cycle of products • Make further progress in the construction and maintenance of waste management infrastructure for cities and regions • Design and implement consumer-targeted initiatives to raise citizens' awareness on waste prevention, separate collection and sustainable consumption • Conclude and implement a regional agreement on the prevention of plastic pollution, including specifically addressing the priority issue of marine litter	• Alignment with EU targets
Waste	National Plan for Integrated Waste Management	2020-35	• Gradual transition from a linear to a circular economy by encouraging waste diversion through waste reuse and recycling • Increase government capacities at the national and local levels • Mobilise finance for waste management • Identify and define the methodology and technology for future waste treatment investments in an integrated waste management system, including equipment for waste collection, composting, recycling, incineration for energy recovery and disposal on the basis of waste management areas • Improve human resources, awareness raising and public participation in waste management	Targets for 2035: • Recycling rate: 40% • Population in urban areas covered by integrated waste management services: 100% • Recovery rate of packaging waste: 70% • Landfilling rate: 10% Targets for 2035 for specific waste streams: • Separate collection: 40% of municipal solid waste • Landfilling rate: maximum of 10% of generated municipal waste • Biodegradable waste: reduction of landfilling of biodegradable waste to 35% of the biodegradable municipal

				solid waste generated in 2016 • Construction and demolition waste: recycle 70% • Packaging: 70% recovery of packaging generated and 60% recovery of total packaging with material-specific targets for paper and cardboard (60%), metals (50%), plastics (22.5%), glass (60%), and wood (15%) • Batteries: recycle 50-70% for different materials • Waste electrical and electronic equipment (WEEE): separate collection > 4 kg per capita of WEEE from private or individual homes annually; recovery between 70% and 80%; recycle between 50% and 75% • Number of centres for the collection of construction and demolition waste: 61
Climate	National Strategy for Climate Change	2020-30	• Alignment with the EU framework on environment and climate to meet Paris Agreement targets • Strengthen the capacity of relevant institutions and inter-institutional co-operation • Ensure sustainable development of the economy • Reduce greenhouse gas (GHG) emissions (with a specific focus on energy, transport, agriculture, and land-use change and forestry) • Set up a monitoring, reporting and verification system of GHGs • Improve waste management by reducing waste generation and increasing recycling • Resilience and adaptation to climate change • Awareness raising on projected climate change impacts	• Reduction of CO_2 emissions by 11.5% by 2030 compared to baseline emissions (2016) – 50 kilotonnes of carbon dioxide (kt CO_2) savings for the construction sector through thermal insulation – 277 kt CO_2 savings for the industry sector through energy efficiency, diversification of fuel – 381 kt CO_2 savings for the transportation sector through cost-effective measures and the introduction of biomass
			Directly related documents	
Sustainable development	National Strategy for Development and Integration	2022-30	• Harmonisation with the Sustainable Development Goals and guide Albania in its EU integration process • Specific priority area on integrated waste management and the circular economy. The aim is to improve waste management infrastructure, meet EU legal targets, and increase public awareness and education in that regard.	• Alignment with the National Plan for Integrated Waste Management
Climate and energy	National Energy and Climate Plan	2021-30	• Steer decarbonisation efforts until 2030 and beyond, aligning with the ambitions of the European Green Deal • Integrate five dimensions of the Energy Union: energy efficiency, renewables, GHG emissions reductions, internal energy market, and research and innovation	• Reduction of GHG emissions by 18.7% by 2030 compared to the business-as-usual scenario • Increase the share of renewable energy in final energy demand up to 54.4% by 2030 • Reduce final energy demand by 8.4% by 2030
Private sector	Business Investment and Development	2021-27	• Strengthen Albania's enterprise and industrial policy, in particular small and medium-sized enterprises' skills	None directly related to the transition to a circular economy

	Strategy		development, innovation, sustainable growth and conditions for attracting foreign investment • Specific focus on the circular transition: promoting changes in supply chains for more sustainable and circular products and services • Empowerment of the start-up ecosystem, with a special emphasis given to products and services that contribute to the development of the green economy • Strong push for eco-innovation through financial incentives • Upscale of skills development in "green" sectors and jobs • Promotion of investments for the green economy • Awareness-raising campaigns on the opportunities of the green and circular transition	
Tourism	National Strategy for Sustainable Tourism Development	2019-23	• Create new development poles and industries and consolidate the tourism offer • Increase the added value of tourism potentials for the economic and social development of the country • Development of new products and services in tourism, as well as improvement of their quality • Improve the country's image and promotion of local products • Focus on three sectors: coastal (maritime), natural (mountain tourism, eco-tourism, waterfront, environmentally protected areas) and thematic (culture, agritourism, event and business, eno-gastronomy, health)	• Increasing tourism's direct contribution to gross domestic product from 8.4% in 2016 to 10% in 2023 and the total contribution from 26% in 2016 to 29% in 2023 • Increasing the incoming tourism revenue from EUR 1.7 billion in 2017 to EUR 2 billion in 2023

Waste management

Waste management in Albania is covered in the amended Laws on Environmental Protection and on Integrated Waste Management, both adopted in 2011. Several decisions of the Council of Ministers cover specific waste streams (both municipal and industrial) and specify the competencies of central and local governments. While the Law on Integrated Waste Management envisaged the transposition of EU waste legislation, it pre-dates the revisions of the EU Waste Framework Directive adopted in 2018.

Promisingly, after being delayed since 2020, Albania amended its waste management law to ban the use of certain categories of plastic bags[23] in March 2022 and has partially aligned with the EU Directive on single-use plastics. Further alignment with this directive is needed, by banning other single-use plastic items (European Commission, 2022[84]). A task force was established following the adoption of the amendment to ensure enforcement of the ban.

To ensure alignment with the Waste Framework Directive, the Albanian government is in the process of further revising its legislative framework, through acts transposing the European List of Wastes into Albanian legislation. Regarding the producer responsibility organisations, the new Law on Extended Producer Responsibility (EPR), which aims to establish the schemes[24] for the collection and recycling of special waste streams, such as packaging waste, waste from electronic and electrical equipment, and waste from batteries and accumulators, has been drafted[25] and is expected to be adopted in the second quarter of 2024. The draft EPR Law foresees the product tax coming into effect in January 2025, with 30% of all income generated going into a Special Fund for Circular Economy.

The draft EPR Law largely covers aspects of the OECD EPR Guidance (see Chapter 4) (OECD, 2016[88]). Outlined rules pertain to the creation and functioning of producer responsibility organisations, spanning their authorisation process as well as the registry of data related to products under EPR, producers or the producer responsibility organisation itself. They also clearly define the responsible institutions (national and local government) as well as co-ordination among them for the implementation of the law, alongside the obligations (e.g. reporting) and sanctions against non-compliance of registered producers or producer responsibility organisations. In the case of Albania, the National Environmental Agency will be responsible for the inspection and monitoring of EPR schemes.

Two main strategic documents have been adopted covering waste, in 2019 and 2020, respectively: the National Plan for Integrated Waste Management (NPIWM) (2020-2035), which covers both municipal and industrial waste, and the National Sectorial Plan for Solid Waste Management (2019-2035).

The NPIWM (2020-2035) was developed based on the results of the previous NPIWM (2011-2019), whose ambitious measures and targets were largely not implemented or achieved (e.g. increase the amount of waste collected by local authorities that is recycled or mixed to 55% by 2020, starting from a very low base and with underdeveloped separation-at-source infrastructure) mostly due to the overall lack of staff and financial resources to ensure greater enforcement (OECD, 2021[13]).

The NPIWM envisages a gradual transition from a linear to a circular economy by encouraging waste diversion from landfills to waste reuse and recycling through improved waste separation at source. Its main objectives are to:

- Improve waste management by meeting the main targets and legal requirements. This includes establishing efficient systems for measuring and reporting municipal waste, drafting local municipal plans, improving the collection and treatment of waste based on the waste hierarchy, closing non-compliant landfills, and implementing EPR schemes.
- Improve and harmonise the legal framework for waste management. This includes clarifying institutional roles and responsibilities for central and local governments and developing guidelines for municipalities.
- Mobilise sustainable financing of waste management, including infrastructure. Municipalities will be tasked to determine their budgetary needs for the complete cycle of waste management and related fees.
- Improve human resources and citizens' awareness of and participation in waste management. Expertise on green public procurement will be supported. Awareness-raising campaigns and educational courses promoting waste reduction and sustainable consumption will be organised.

The current NPIWM specifies more realistic targets, set over three periods, with goals for 2025, 2030 and 2035[26] (see Table 2.1) with defined institutions responsible for their implementation. Monitoring and evaluation are set to be conducted annually, and data collection is to be improved to measure performance against the targets.

To reach these objectives, a number of activities are ongoing (EEA, 2021[71]):

- Preparation of local waste management plans for some municipalities.
- Improvement of the infrastructure in some municipalities (bins, vehicles) and pilot projects on separate collection.
- Improvement of the waste data management system by providing verified data on municipal waste and the potential for GHG reductions with support from international development co-operation partners. A weighting exercise has been conducted in all municipalities as part of the project.

- The National Environmental Agency is implementing a nationwide campaign to raise the awareness of the general public and educate local institutions with regard to waste management services (the ban of single-use plastic items is one of the topics discussed). The campaign has been realised in all 61 municipalities. Municipalities also organise the "Let's do it" public awareness campaigns promoting responsible environmental behaviour and waste reduction, reuse and recycling.
- Start of the rehabilitation and closure of some existing dumpsites.
- Start of feasibility studies for two waste management zones, which would be the base units for integrated waste management planning: Fier and Elbasan. These zones are to include at least one centre for the recovery of recyclable and compostable materials, an incinerator with energy recovery, or a sanitary landfill.
- Establishment of three composting facilities and three material recovery facilities.

The National Sectorial Plan for Solid Waste Management is a detailed investment plan for local and regional solid waste management infrastructure (waste collection and transport, reduction and recycling of waste, treatment, and disposal facilities) for the period 2019-35.

Climate action

Albania strengthened its climate action policy framework with the adoption of the National Climate Change Strategy and corresponding national mitigation and adaptation plans in 2019. The main objectives of the strategy are relevant to a circular economy transition and include:

- Reducing GHG emissions, mainly from the transport sector and energy production.
- Promoting renewable energy, in particular solar, wind and hydropower.
- Enhancing energy efficiency, in particular in buildings and transportation. This includes promoting energy-efficient technologies and encouraging less energy consumption.
- Improving waste management by reducing waste generation and increasing recycling.
- Strengthening Albania's resilience to the impacts of climate change, namely floods, droughts and extreme weather events. This includes improving infrastructure, enhancing early warning systems and promoting agriculture practices.

Albania submitted its revised Nationally Determined Contribution (NDC) to the United Nations Framework Convention on Climate Change in 2021. The NDCs acknowledge that climate change is a cross-cutting issue for all sectors in Albania, and that several policies and strategies have or are being developed to address it. The NDCs are complemented by an Action Plan, which builds on the National Climate Change Strategy, through the integration of its priority actions, and by aligning implementation mechanisms and timelines.

Moreover, Albania is one of the two economies in the Western Balkans (along with North Macedonia) that has adopted its National Energy and Climate Plan in 2021, as mandated by the Energy Community. Nevertheless, crucial improvements are necessary to ensure the plan is successfully leading the economy towards achieving 2030 climate targets. In particular, the plan lacks ambition in reducing GHG emissions and many of the envisaged policies lack an operationalisation plan with concrete funding sources and timelines (Climate Action Network Europe, 2022[89]).

Industry

The Country Programme for Inclusive and Sustainable Industrial Development in Albania was developed as a comprehensive programmatic framework to achieve inclusive and sustainable industrial development for the period 2020-24. It includes around 20 project proposals in 3 priority areas: 1) industrial competitiveness and market access; 2) productive employment and entrepreneurship development; and

3) sustainable energy for productive uses and environmental management (UNIDO, 2020[90]). The identified components are aligned with the Sustainable Development Goals (SDGs) and some programmes are planned to boost the circular economy. For instance, one of the projects strives to transform the market for using organic waste from olive oil production and other industries for energy generation. The programme also envisages the development of eco-industrial parks; however, this measure had not been implemented at the time of writing (De Oliveira Pereira, 2019[91]).

A Zero Draft Roadmap on Sustainability and Resource Use in the Textiles, Clothing, Leather, and Footwear industries of Albania was launched in October 2022 within the framework of the Business Partnerships and Solutions for SDGs, a project funded and implemented by international co-operation partners. The overall objective of the roadmap is to improve the sustainability of the textiles, clothing, leather and footwear sector in Albania with evidence on its environmental, social and economic impacts and to work with a wide range of stakeholders across the supply chain to support the transition to formality and fill existing sector gaps regarding waste collection, separation, recycling, energy efficiency and water treatment (ILO and UNIDO, 2023[21]).

The Non-Food Industry Strategy (2016-2025), active between 2016 and 2019, prioritised enhancing competitiveness in sectors dealing with raw materials, mineral resources and waste. While not explicitly centered on circularity, the strategy focused on optimising natural resource use and integrating secondary raw materials into production processes to alleviate environmental impact. The strategy planned to apply best available techniques for modernised production in areas like metal ore, non-metallic minerals processing and waste management, aiming to reduce energy use and promote recycled materials to minimise environmental harm. Another key aspect of the strategy was the revival of historic industrial sites in various locations like Elbasan, Fier, Lac, Rubik, Shkoder and Burrel to attract both local and foreign investments. The goal was to enhance the non-food industry's impact on Albania's GDP, exports and employment rates. The strategy also proposed initiatives for the remediation of contaminated industrial sites and the construction of infrastructure for managing industrial waste, particularly hazardous waste.

Private sector

The legal and policy framework targeting private sector and industrial development has recently been strengthened to improve the business environment; with circular economy policies being increasingly recognised in some strategic documents.

The newly adopted Law on Support and Development of Start-ups (2022) and its related measures aim to support the innovation ecosystem, are expected to facilitate peer-to-peer learning and the development of products and services that contribute to a green and circular economy.

The new Business Investment and Development Strategy (2021-2027) has a specific focus on the circular transition, as part of the "green and digital transformation" pillar. In particular, it encourages companies to increasingly make changes in their supply chains as a response to opportunities that more sustainable and circular products and services could bring. A stronger push for eco-innovation in the post-COVID economic recovery is envisaged through awareness-raising and capacity-building activities as well as improved access to green finance, such as through the provision of grants for eco-innovative start-ups, government credit guarantee schemes for green projects, the development of a network of business angels and regulation of crowd funding. Trainings and educational programmes are planned to upscale skills development in this regard. For instance, the Albanian Development Guarantee Foundation has a "green window" to support SMEs and investments in the agriculture sector that aim to reduce energy consumption or CO_2 emissions by at least 20%. As of December 2022, the foundation had guaranteed 42 green loans for a total of EUR 3 million.

Albania has also made some progress in developing a Smart Specialisation Strategy, with the establishment of an Inter-Ministerial Committee overseeing its drafting and implementation. A national team on smart specialisation was also created as a technical-level structure, comprised of experts and representatives from various institutions and organisations (S3 Platform, 2024[92]). A roadmap has been completed, and the Entrepreneurial Discovery Process, in line with the European Commission's Joint Research Centre methodology, started in 2022. Following the development of quantitative and qualitative mapping of Albania's economic, innovative, scientific and technological potential, preliminary priorities have been identified. Circular economy considerations could be highly relevant to some of the key preliminary priorities, encompassing sectors such as agriculture, forestry, and fishing; manufacturing; energy; as well as accommodation and supporting service activities. The circular economy could be included as a horizontal objective. This would imply promoting the circular economy as a cross-cutting priority across all sectors and areas of focus outlined in the strategy. By systematically incorporating all aspects of economic development, innovation and policy making to foster a more sustainable and resilient economy, Albania could maximise resource use while minimising environmental impact and generating long-term socio-economic benefits.

Moreover, recognition of green best practices through eco-labelling, which can encourage the production, marketing and use of products with a reduced impact on the environment, is legislated in Albania (Regulation on the Approval of the Procedure and Criteria for Granting an Eco-label, Its Use and Validity; as well as the composition and functioning of the Commission for the Issue of Eco-label). Nevertheless, while the legislation requests the Ministry of Tourism and Environment to adopt guidelines on the criteria for granting eco-labels for each product or product group, only one guideline on textiles has been developed to date. A certification body responsible for delivering eco-labels is yet to be established in Albania.

Public procurement

The public procurement market in Albania represented 10.7% of the country's GDP in 2021, having more than doubled from a share of 4.8% in 2019, mainly driven by post-earthquake reconstruction projects and economic contraction caused by the COVID-19 pandemic (European Commission, 2022[93]). Given the major role the public sector plays in driving the demand for products and services, it is a powerful tool for the circular transition in Albania.

The Public Procurement Law (2020) mandates contracting authorities to adhere to environmental, social and labour legislation. It also allows the consideration of climate impacts in the awarding criteria (OECD, 2022[46]). The Public Procurement Agency published a Green Procurement Roadmap and general methodology in 2023. While Albania introduced its National Public Procurement Strategy 2020-2023 in 2020, no specific advancements in green procurement legislation have been made. The legal framework for public procurement should be enhanced to integrate circularity-related sustainability concerns, like resource efficiency, waste reduction and eco-friendly product development, into public procurement processes. By considering these factors in awarding contracts, the law would encourage the purchase of goods and services that promote circular practices, contributing to a more sustainable and circular economy in Albania. The revision status of the National Public Procurement Strategy 2020-2023 is currently unknown.

Tourism

The National Strategy for Sustainable Tourism Development (2019-2023) was the first tourism strategy adopted after ministries in charge of tourism and environment joined forces to form the Ministry of Tourism and Environment in 2017. The strategy outlines the government's objectives for the tourism sector, in particular promoting sustainable tourism, improving infrastructure and services, and creating a favourable business environment for tourism operators. Although the strategy does not specifically cover the circular economy, it includes a range of measures to develop sustainable tourism practices that minimise negative impacts on the environment and preserve Albania's natural and cultural assets.

The Ministry of Tourism and Environment is in the process of drafting the new tourism strategy for the period 2024-30, which will focus on high-end and eco-tourism. The planned objective of the strategy going forward will not be to attract more tourists, but to diversify the tourism offer and attract tourists for longer stays and all year round to reduce pressures on coastal areas and develop better services. Some of the touristic destinations planned to be promoted include mountains, forests and the coastline, with a focus on cultural heritage, gastronomy, hiking and rafting. The strategy plans to develop a long-term, resilient, sustainable tourism industry, respectful of destinations' natural and social ecosystems, and include circular economy aspects.

Overview of circular economy initiatives and main non-governmental stakeholders in Albania

A number of stakeholders have been involved in different circular economy-related activities and initiatives in Albania. They focus on different aspects relevant for the circular economy – primarily, though, on waste management and awareness-raising activities. However, their work remains uncoordinated, and synergies remain to be created between them. Figure 2.14 provides an overview of the main non-governmental circular economy stakeholders in Albania.

Figure 2.14. Overview of the main non-governmental circular economy stakeholders in Albania

Note: The list in non-exhaustive.

The community of international development co-operation partners is conducting several projects relevant for the circular economy in Albania, providing financial and technical support to the government in different areas. Albania's main partners and international development co-operation partners include the European Union, the Swiss Agency for Development and Cooperation, Kreditanstalt für Wiederaufbau (KfW), Deutsche Gesellschaft für Internationale Zusammenarbeit (GIZ), the French Development Agency, the World Bank and United Nations agencies (see Annex C for an overview of non-governmental stakeholders). The majority of projects undertaken by the international community aim at strengthening municipal and industrial waste management (enhanced infrastructure, waste prevention activities, introduction of waste recycling programmes) (see Annex B). While some initiatives include grants and subsidies, buy-in from the private sector remains limited and phase-out processes often lack.

Non-governmental organisations in Albania have been active in promoting and raising awareness on environment- and ecology-related concepts and practices, with some undertaking projects directly focusing on the transition to a circular economy. Some non-governmental organisations have conducted research on the circular economy in Albania (Build Green Group, Environmental & Territorial Management Institute, Urban Research Institute), raised awareness on circular economy concepts (Centre for Competitiveness Skills, Co-PLAN Institute for Habitat Development, Environmental Centre for Development Education and

Networking), developed platforms to connect circular economy businesses (Circular Economy Club Tirana, Build Green Group), and implemented projects on circular waste management (Institute for Environmental Policy, Milieukontakt) (see Annex C). Nevertheless, their initiatives remain uncoordinated and are rarely led by a strategic government approach towards the circular transition.

Academia and research institutes have also been at the forefront of conducting analyses and developing solutions to increase the uptake of circular economy practices. Several universities in Albania (such as the University of Tirana, the Agricultural University of Tirana, the Polytechnic University of Tirana and Polis University) offer courses introducing circular economy concepts (see Annex C). Nevertheless, while the Ministry of Tourism and Environment is undertaking measures to include environment and recycling aspects in school curricula, no concrete initiatives have been taken to develop an overarching circular economy educational programme at the university level.

Private sector organisations, including chambers of commerce, export associations and sector-specific unions, are essential for reaching a wide range of businesses, in particular SMEs. Through awareness-raising activities, conferences and networking events, private sector organisations are increasingly influencing Albanian companies to develop or transition to circular business models (see Annex C).

Several companies in Albania have circular business models, promoting different ways of producing and consuming goods and services. The main circular businesses in Albania focus on the reuse of agricultural surplus and by-products, sustainable packaging options, and recycled waste (particularly from vehicles or electronics) (see Annex C). While their contribution is required to transition to a more resource-efficient and circular economy, government measures have rarely supported them financially or technically. Moreover, as the vast majority of businesses are still not familiar with circular concepts, it remains difficult to map all the actors concerned.

References

AIDA (2022), "Tourism", https://aida.gov.al/en/business-in-albania/sectors/tourism. [10]

Albanian Government (2020), *Karavasta Photovoltaic Park, biggest investment in solar power in Balkans*, https://www.kryeministria.al/en/newsroom/parku-fotovoltaik-i-karavastase-investimi-me-i-madh-ne-ballkan-per-energjine-diellore/. [95]

Altax (2019), "Oil industry in figures in Albania", https://altax.al/en/1-oil-industry-in-figures-in-albania-2019. [58]

Climate Action Network Europe (2022), "Two years after Sofia: Limited progress of national climate and energy plans in the Western Balkans, new report by CAN Europe warns", press release, https://caneurope.org/wb-necp-report-2022. [89]

Crippa, M. et al. (2023), *CO2 Emissions of All World Countries*, Publications Office of the European Union, Luxembourg, https://edgar.jrc.ec.europa.eu/booklet/GHG_emissions_of_all_world_countries_booklet_2023report.pdf. [53]

Dalberg Advisors, WWF Mediterranean Marine Initiative (2019), *Stop the Flood of Plastic: How Mediterranean Countries Can Save Their Sea*, World Wide Fund for Nature, https://www.wwf.fr/sites/default/files/doc-2019-06/20190607_Rapport_Stoppons_le_torrent_de_plastique_WWF-min.pdf. [76]

De Oliveira Pereira, D. (2019), “Bioenergy that is good for business”, https://www.unido.org/stories/bioenergy-good-business (accessed on 11 January 2023). [91]

Design4Circle (2021), *Circular Economy in the Textile and Footwear Industry: Skills and Competences for a Sector Renewal*, Design4Circle, https://design4circle.eu/wp-content/uploads/2021/04/CIRCULAR%20ECONOMY_IN_THE_TEXTILE_AND_FOOTWEAR_INDUSTRY_SKILLS_COMPETENCIES_FOR_SECTORAL_RENEWAL.pdf. [23]

EEA (2022), “Waste recycling in Europe”, https://www.eea.europa.eu/ims/waste-recycling-in-europe. [74]

EEA (2021), *Municipal Waste Management in Western Balkan Countries: Albania*, European Environment Agency, Copenhagen, https://www.eea.europa.eu/themes/waste/waste-management/municipal-waste-management-country/albania-municipal-waste-factsheet-2021/#:~:text=Albania%20has%20a%20new%20national,the%20treatment%20of%20residual%20MSW. [71]

EEA (2018), *Municipal Waste Management: Albania – Country Fact Sheet*, European Environment Agency, Copenhagen, https://www.eea.europa.eu/themes/waste/waste-management/municipal-waste-management-country-profiles/albania-municipal-waste-factsheet-2018. [85]

Einarsson, S. and F. Sorin (2020), *Circular Economy in Travel and Tourism: A Conceptual Framework for a Sustainable, Resilent and Future Proof Industry Transition*, CE360 Alliance, https://circulareconomy.europa.eu/platform/sites/default/files/circular-economy-in-travel-and-tourism.pdf. [17]

EIT Raw Materials (2021), *Roadmap of Actions for the Exploitation of RM Sector in the ESEE Region*, EIT Raw Materials, https://reseerve.eu/upload/content/446/d6-4-final_executive-summary_web.pdf. [87]

EIU (2022), *What to Watch in the Western Balkans in 2023*, Economist Intelligence Unit, London, https://viewpoint.eiu.com/analysis/article/422592625. [12]

Environment Go (2022), “Top natural rescources in Albania”, https://environmentgo.com/10-top-natural-resources-in-albania. [62]

European Commission (2023), “Agriculture in the enlargement countries”, https://agriculture.ec.europa.eu/international/international-cooperation/enlargement/candidates_en (accessed on 31 October 2023). [38]

European Commission (2022), *2022 Communication on EU Enlargement Policy: Albania Progress Report*, European Commission, Brussels, https://neighbourhood-enlargement.ec.europa.eu/system/files/2022-10/Albania%20Report%202022.pdf. [84]

European Commission (2022), *Albania 2022 Report*, European Commission, Brussels, https://neighbourhood-enlargement.ec.europa.eu/system/files/2022-10/Albania%20Report%202022.pdf. [93]

European Commission (2022), *Annual Report on European SMEs 2021/2022*, European Commission, Brussels, https://ec.europa.eu/docsroom/documents/50654/attachments/1/translations/en/renditions/native#:~:text=However%2C%20due%20to%20their%20large,greenhouse%20gas%20emissions%20by%20enterprises. [49]

European Commission (2022), *EU Candidate Countries' & Potential Candidates' Economic Quarterly (CCEQ) – Western Balkans and Türkiye. 3rd Quarter 2022*, European Commission, Brussels, https://doi.org/10.2765/418856. [3]

European Commission (2020), *Green Agenda for the Western Balkans*, European Commission, Brussels, https://neighbourhood-enlargement.ec.europa.eu/system/files/2020-10/green_agenda_for_the_western_balkans_en.pdf. [77]

European Commission (2020), "The impact of textile production and waste on the environment (infographics)", https://www.europarl.europa.eu/news/en/headlines/society/20201208STO93327/the-impact-of-textile-production-and-waste-on-the-environment-infographics (accessed on 4 December 2023). [22]

Eurostat (2023), "Energy statistics", https://ec.europa.eu/eurostat/statistics-explained/index.php?title=Energy_statistics_-_an_overview (accessed on 2 November 2023). [55]

Eurostat (2023), "Energy statistics: An overview", https://ec.europa.eu/eurostat/statistics-explained/index.php?title=Energy_statistics_-_an_overview. [57]

Eurostat (2023), "Enlargement countries – energy statistics", https://ec.europa.eu/eurostat/statistics-explained/index.php?title=Enlargement_countries_-_energy_statistics#Energy_trade (accessed on 6 November 2023). [60]

Eurostat (2023), "Expenditure by duration, purpose, main destination of the trip and expenditure category", https://ec.europa.eu/eurostat/databrowser/view/tour_dem_extot/default/table?lang=en (accessed on 10 January 2024). [16]

Eurostat (2023), "Gross value added and income by A*10 industry breakdowns", https://ec.europa.eu/eurostat/databrowser/view/nama_10_a10__custom_8247007/default/table (accessed on 6 December 2023). [6]

Eurostat (2023), "Treatment of waste by waste category, hazardousness and waste management", https://ec.europa.eu/eurostat/databrowser/view/env_wastrt/default/table?lang=en (accessed on 25 November 2023). [80]

Eurostat (2022), "EU energy mix and import dependency (archive)", https://ec.europa.eu/eurostat/statistics-explained/index.php?title=EU_energy_mix_and_import_dependency#Energy_mix_and_import_dependency. [59]

Eurostat (2022), "GDP, current prices", https://ec.europa.eu/eurostat/databrowser/view/nama_10_gdp/default/table?lang=en (accessed on 25 November 2023). [69]

Eurostat (2022), "Material flow accounts and resource productivity", https://ec.europa.eu/eurostat/databrowser/view/env_ac_rp/default/table?lang=en. [63]

Eurostat (2021), "Municipal waste statistics", https://ec.europa.eu/eurostat/databrowser/view/env_wasmun/default/table?lang=en (accessed on 6 December 2023). [70]

Eurostat (2020), "Small and medium-sized enterprises: An overview", https://ec.europa.eu/eurostat/web/products-eurostat-news/-/ddn-20200514-1 (accessed on 1 December 2023). [47]

Extractive Industries Transparency Initiative (2020), *Extractive Industries Transparency Initiative Albania: Report for the Years 2017 and 2018*, Deloitte Audit Albania, Tirana, https://eiti.org/sites/default/files/attachments/eiti-draft-report-2017-2018.pdf. [32]

Gjonaj, A. (2020), "The mining rent is zeroed: The aim is to curb the export of low-value raw ore", Albanian Telegraphic Agency, https://ata.gov.al/2020/11/07/zerohet-renta-minerare-synohet-frenimi-i-eksportimit-te-mineralit-bruto-te-paperpunuar-me-vlere-te-ulet. [34]

ICT (2021), *SME Competitiveness Outlook 2021: Empowering the Green Recovery*, International Trade Centre, Geneva, https://www.intracen.org/publications/smeco2021/ITCSMECO2021. [48]

ILO and UNIDO (2023), *SDG Principles and Positive Practices Adopted by the Textile, Clothing, Leather, and Footwear Sector in Albania*, International Labour Organization, Geneva, https://www.ilo.org/wcmsp5/groups/public/---europe/---ro-geneva/---sro-budapest/documents/publication/wcms_869582.pdf. [21]

INSTAT (2023), *Agriculture Statistics 2022*, Institute of Statistics, Tirana, https://www.instat.gov.al/media/11772/agriculture-statistics-2022.pdf. [43]

INSTAT (2023), "Construction figures", https://www.instat.gov.al/en/themes/industry-trade-and-services/construction (accessed on 10 January 2024). [25]

INSTAT (2023), *Employment in Albania*, https://www.instat.gov.al/en/statistical-literacy/employment-in-albania (accessed on 6 December 2023). [9]

INSTAT (2023), *Indicators by economic activities by economic activity, type and year*, http://databaza.instat.gov.al/pxweb/en/DST/START__NA__NAY__NAYPA/NAYPA2/table/tableViewLayout1 (accessed on 6 December 2023). [28]

INSTAT (2023), "International trade in goods", http://databaza.instat.gov.al/pxweb/en/DST/START__FT__FTE/NewFTE005/table/tableViewLayout1 (accessed on 10 January 2024). [19]

INSTAT (2023), "Managed waste origin by type and year", http://databaza.instat.gov.al/pxweb/en/DST/START__EN__MU/MU11/table/tableViewLayout1 (accessed on 25 November 2023). [78]

INSTAT (2023), *Material Flow Accounts*, Institute of Statistics, Tirana, https://www.instat.gov.al/media/11487/material-flow-accounts-2021.pdf. [66]

INSTAT (2023), *Statistics on Small and Medium Enterprises, 2021*, Institute of Statistics, Tirana, https://www.instat.gov.al/media/11356/results-on-sme-2021.pdf. [45]

INSTAT (2023), "Total generated waste by type and year", http://databaza.instat.gov.al/pxweb/en/DST/START__EN__MU/MU04 (accessed on 2 November 2023). [82]

INSTAT (2023), "Urban waste in tonnes by urban waste treatment, type and year", http://databaza.instat.gov.al/pxweb/en/DST/START__EN__MU/MU05 (accessed on 2 November 2023). [83]

INSTAT (2023), "Value by country, group of commodities, import/export, type and year", http://databaza.instat.gov.al/pxweb/en/DST/START__FT__FTY/NewFTY007/table/tableViewLayout1 (accessed on 7 November 2023). [41]

INSTAT (2023), "Value by gruppro, economic activity, import/export, type and year", http://databaza.instat.gov.al/pxweb/en/DST/START__FT__FTE/NewFTE005/table/tableViewLayout1 (accessed on 25 November 2023). [29]

INSTAT (2022), *Albania Institute of Statistics*, http://databaza.instat.gov.al/pxweb/en/DST/?rxid=ab6a42a1-79b5-4ddd-aea6-829a85e396e1. [67]

INSTAT (2022), *Urban Solid Waste, 2022*, Institute of Statistics, Tirana, https://www.instat.gov.al/media/12579/urban-solid-waste-2022.pdf. [79]

Invest in Albania (2023), "Invest in agriculture in Albania", web page, https://invest-in-albania.org/industries/agriculture. [37]

Invest in Albania (n.d.), "Cloth manufacturing – The textile industry in Albania", web page, https://invest-in-albania.org/industries/clothing-manufacturing (accessed on 6 February 2023). [20]

IRENA (2021), *Renewables Readiness Assessment – Albania*, International Renewable Energy Agency, Abu Dhabi, https://www.irena.org/-/media/Files/IRENA/Agency/Publication/2021/March/IRENA_RRA_Albania_2021.pdf. [64]

JRC/IEA (2023), *Country Fact Sheet Albania*, EDGAR – Emissions Database for Global Atmospheric Research, https://edgar.jrc.ec.europa.eu/country_profile/ALB (accessed on 2 November 2023). [54]

KESH (2023), "Skavica Project", web page, https://www.kesh.al/en/skavica-project. [94]

Ministry of Agriculture and Rural Development (2023), "Record value of 55.1 billion lek agricultural exports in 2022", https://bujqesia.gov.al/vlere-rekord-prej-5-1-mld-leke-eksporte-bujqesore-ne-vitin-2022 (accessed on 31 October 2023). [42]

Ministry of Agriculture and Rural Development (2022), *Rural Development Programme of the Republic of Albania*, Ministry of Agriculture and Rural Development, Tirana, https://bujqesia.gov.al/wp-content/uploads/2022/09/Programi-IPARD-III_2021-2027_English.pdf. [36]

Ministry of Infrastructure and Energy (2023), *Register of Active Mining Permits February 2023*, Ministry of Infrastructure and Energy, Tirana, http://www.akbn.gov.al/regjistri-i-lejeve-minerare-aktive-shkurt-2023. [31]

Ministry of Infrastructure and Energy (2016), *Development of the Non-Food Industry Strategy, 2016-2025*, Ministry of Infrastructure and Energy, Tirana, https://www.infrastruktura.gov.al/wp-content/uploads/2017/10/DOKUMENTI_STRATEGJIK_I_POLITIKAVE_TE_INDUSTRISE_JO_USHQIMORE._18_Pri.pdf. [27]

Ministry of Tourism and Environment (2022), *The Fourth National Communication of Albania on Climate Change*, Ministry of Tourism and Environment, Tirana, https://unfccc.int/sites/default/files/resource/Fourth%20National%20Communication%20of%20Albania%20to%20the%20UNFCCC_EN.pdf. [52]

Ministry of Tourism and Environment (2020), *National Integrated Waste Management Plan 2020-2035*, Ministry of Tourism and Environment, Tirana. [81]

Ministry of Tourism and Environment (2019), *National Climate Change Strategy*, Ministry of Tourism and Environment, Tirana, https://turizmi.gov.al/wp-content/uploads/2021/10/2.-Strategjia-e-Ndryshimeve-Klimatike-dhe-Planet-e-Veprimit_Qershor-2019_-1.pdf. [40]

National Agency of Natural Resources (2022), *Invest in Albanian Natural Resources*, National Agency of Natural Resources, Tirana, http://www.akbn.gov.al/wp-content/uploads/2022/10/Mineral-Resources-20222.pdf. [30]

National Agency of Natural Resources (2022), "Mineral resources", in *Invest in Albanian Natural Resources*, National Agency of Natural Resources, Tirana, http://www.akbn.gov.al/wp-content/uploads/2022/10/Mineral-Resources-20222.pdf. [33]

National Environmental Agency (2022), *Report on the Status of the Environment 2022*, National Environment Agency, Tirana, https://akm.gov.al/ova_doc/raporti-per-gjendjen-e-mjedisit-2022 (accessed on 7 November 2023). [72]

OECD (2024), *Value added by activity* (indicator), https://doi.org/10.1787/a8b2bd2b-en (accessed on 19 February 2024). [8]

OECD (2023), "Inflation (CPI)", https://data.oecd.org/price/inflation-cpi.htm (accessed on 22 November 2023). [5]

OECD (2023), "Real GDP forecast", https://data.oecd.org/gdp/real-gdp-forecast.htm (accessed on 6 December 2023). [4]

OECD (2022), *Municipal Waste, Generation and Treatment Database*, https://stats.oecd.org/index.aspx?DataSetCode=MUNW (accessed on 25 November 2023). [73]

OECD (2022), *SME Policy Index: Western Balkans and Turkey 2022: Assessing the Implementation of the Small Business Act for Europe*, SME Policy Index, OECD Publishing, Paris, https://doi.org/10.1787/b47d15f0-en. [46]

OECD (2021), *Competitiveness in South East Europe 2021: A Policy Outlook*, Competitiveness and Private Sector Development, OECD Publishing, Paris, https://doi.org/10.1787/dcbc2ea9-en. [13]

OECD (2021), *Facilitating the Green Transition for ASEANS SMEs: A Toolkit for Policymakers*, OECD, Paris, https://www.oecd.org/southeast-asia/regional-programme/networks/Facilitating-green-%20transition-for-ASEAN-SMEs.pdf. [50]

OECD (2021), "No net zero without SMEs: Exploring the key issues for greening SMEs and green entrepreneurship", *OECD SME and Entrepreneurship Papers*, No. 30, OECD Publishing, Paris, https://doi.org/10.1787/bab63915-en. [24]

OECD (2021), *Towards a More Resource-efficient and Circular Economy: The Role of the G20*, OECD, Paris, https://www.oecd.org/environment/waste/OECD-G20-Towards-a-more-Resource-Efficient-and-Circular-Economy.pdf. [68]

OECD (2019), *Circular Approach and the Sustainability of the Agro-food System – Closing Resource Loops to Improve Sustainability*, OECD, Paris, https://web-archive.oecd.org/2021-07-26/503775-circular-approach-and-the-sustainability-of-the-agro-food-system-3-april-2019.htm. [44]

OECD (2019), *Global Material Resources Outlook to 2060: Economic Drivers and Environmental Consequences*, OECD Publishing, Paris, https://doi.org/10.1787/9789264307452-en. [65]

OECD (2016), *Extended Producer Responsibility: Updated Guidance for Efficient Waste Management*, OECD Publishing, Paris, https://doi.org/10.1787/9789264256385-en. [88]

Pennington, J. (2022), "3 ways the circular economy is vital for the energy transition", World Economic Forum, https://www.weforum.org/agenda/2022/02/3-ways-circular-economy-renewables-energy-transition. [61]

RCC (2023), *Balkan Business Barometer Opinion 2023*, Regional Cooperation Council, Sarajevo, https://www.rcc.int/balkanbarometer/results/1/business. [51]

Ritchie, H., M. Roser and P. Rosado (2022), *CO2 and Greenhouse Gas Emissions*, Our World in Data, https://ourworldindata.org/co2-and-other-greenhouse-gas-emissions. [56]

S3 Platform (2024), "Smart Specialisation in Albania", https://s3platform.jrc.ec.europa.eu/albania (accessed on 22 January 2024). [92]

Thanas, J., A. Bode and S. Mati (2022), "Mineral waste, recycling and rehabilitation of their disposal areas", *Mining Review*, Vol. 28/2, pp. 37-41, https://doi.org/10.2478/minrv-2022-0012. [86]

UNDP (2022), *Tourism and Hospitality in Albania 2022: An Assessment of Tourism Trends and Performance*, United Nations Development Programme, Nairobi, https://www.undp.org/sites/g/files/zskgke326/files/2022-12/HOSPITALITY%20AND%20TOURISM%20IN%20ALBANIA_FINAL.pdf. [15]

UNECE (2018), *Environmental Performance Reviews: Albania – Third Review Synopsis*, United Nations, New York and Geneva, https://unece.org/DAM/env/epr/epr_studies/Synopsis/Albania_ECE.CEP.183_Synopsis.pdf. [35]

UNIDO (2020), *The Country Programme (CP) for Inclusive and Sustainable Industrial Development for Albania (2020-2024)*, United Nations Industrial Development Organization, https://downloads.unido.org/ot/18/99/18998180/CP%20Albania%20Factsheet_Oct%202020.pdf. [90]

UNWTO (2023), *World Tourism Barometer*, Vol. 21/1, World Tourism Organization, https://webunwto.s3.eu-west-1.amazonaws.com/s3fs-public/2023-01/UNWTO_Barom23_01_January_EXCERPT.pdf?VersionId=_2bbK5GIwk5KrBGJZt5iNPAGnrWoH8NB. [11]

UNWTO (n.d.), *UNWTO Tourism Data Dashboard*, https://www.unwto.org/tourism-data/unwto-tourism-dashboard. [14]

World Bank (2024), *GDP per capita, PPP (constant 2017 international $) - Albania*, https://data.worldbank.org/indicator/NY.GDP.PCAP.PP.KD?locations=AL (accessed on 25 November 2023). [1]

World Bank (2023), "GDP growth (annual %) – Albania", https://data.worldbank.org/indicator/NY.GDP.MKTP.KD.ZG?end=2022&locations=AL&start=1981&view=chart (accessed on 25 November 2023). [2]

World Bank (2023), *Western Balkans Regular Economic Report: Testing Resilience*, World Bank, Washington, DC, https://documents1.worldbank.org/curated/en/099042023104012719/pdf/P179478085f70601a0aac3035c4560691ca.pdf. [26]

World Bank (2022), *Creating Markets in Albania: Taking Advantage of New Trade and Investment Opportunities for a More Robust Private Sector*, International Finance Corporation, Washington, DC, https://www.ifc.org/content/dam/ifc/doc/mgrt/cpsd-albania.pdf. [39]

World Bank (2022), *World Bank National Accounts Data, and OECD National Accounts Data Files*, https://data.worldbank.org/indicator/NV.SRV.TOTL.ZS?locations=OE (accessed on 6 December 2023). [7]

World Bank (2021), "Textiles and clothing (% of value added in manufacturing) – Albania", https://data.worldbank.org/indicator/NV.MNF.TXTL.ZS.UN?locations=AL (accessed on 31 October 2023). [18]

World Bank (2020), *Realizing the Blue Economy Potential in Albania*, World Bank, Washington, DC, https://openknowledge.worldbank.org/server/api/core/bitstreams/0e31273d-a69e-523a-92ec-d49b483daa1c/content. [75]

Notes

[1] The US Virgin Islands ranked as the highest performing destination in 2022.

[2] Forty companies were trained to use computer-aided design/computer-aided manufacture tools in 2023 as part of the "BiznesUP" campaign to integrate digital approaches into business management processes, implemented by GIZ and the Ministry of Finance and Economy.

[3] Adopted in 2019 by the Council of Ministers and implemented by the Ministry of State for Reconstruction for rebuilding and securing residential and public infrastructure, as well as enforcing disaster resilience through improved spatial planning.

[4] The Trans-Adriatic Pipeline, which is connected to the Trans-Anatolian Pipeline, transports natural gas from the Caspian region to Europe. It travels through Greece and Albania, under the Adriatic Sea, to Italy. It crosses Albanian territory predominantly in the Korça region.

[5] The Skavica hydropower plant with a total installed capacity of 210 megawatts (MW) is in its pre-construction phase (KESH, 2023[94]) and concession contracts for the construction of two solar farms with a total installed capacity of 240 MW were approved in 2020 (Albanian Government, 2020[95]).

[6] In Q1 2023, 429 permits were issued, compared to 184 in Q1 2020, 80% of which were for residential construction (INSTAT, 2023[25]).

[7] The Carbon Border Adjustment Mechanism is expected to become operational in 2026 and gradually apply to a selected number of goods with a high risk of carbon leakage (iron and steel, cement, fertiliser, aluminium, and electricity generation). As EU importers will buy carbon certificates corresponding to the carbon price that would have been paid had the goods been produced under EU carbon pricing rules, non-EU producers such as Albania will be encouraged to green their processes and lower production-related emissions.

[8] The data do not, however, cover enterprises in agriculture, forestry and fisheries (INSTAT, 2023[45]).

[9] Albania imported electricity in eight (2011-15, 2017, 2019 and 2020) of the last ten years reported.

[10] Since 2019, two solar auctions have been conducted for a total capacity of 240 MW. Another tender for 300 MW of capacity was launched in 2023 and at least two more are planned in the coming years. Moreover, three bidders have been awarded a total of 222.5 MW in capacity for wind farms at the first wind-power auction in 2023. To assist investors, an analysis of the Albanian territory was conducted to indicate suitable areas for developing solar projects and non-eligible areas for developing wind projects.

[11] The legal procedure requiring environmental impact assessments needed to obtain licences for the construction of hydropower plants has been largely circumvented in Albania, including in protected areas (OECD, 2021[13]).

[12] The European Union currently supplies only 1% of the raw materials needed for key technologies such as wind energy, lithium batteries, silicon photovoltaic assemblies and fuel cells.

[13] Waste data collection was improved in part because INSTAT started gathering data through online questionnaires to municipalities in 2020 and a new methodology was developed in 2021 for collecting and processing waste data. This allowed for more precise estimations on municipal waste generation.

[14] As the Institute of Statistics does not have a definition for “organic waste”, it is not possible to compare the share with the EU bio-waste stream.

[15] As a result of regulatory changes in 2018.

[16] The 2014 regulation on the separate collection of municipal waste at source states that local authorities must organise waste using a three-bin system.

[17] These pilot projects are supported by international development co-operation partners but aim to train municipalities to take over the separation system once the projects end.

[18] Waste pickers are mainly from the Roma community and are ill-equipped and untrained. This activity is not legal in Albania and there are no plans to formalise it.

[19] However, the companies’ ability to effectively process individual materials in large quantity is unknown.

[20] More than 8% of municipal waste generated was not managed in 2022 (INSTAT, 2023[78]).

[21] Incinerators generally operate under contractual agreements that require a minimum amount of waste to be provided, which can limit the availability of recyclable materials for recycling companies, thus impacting the overall effectiveness of recycling efforts.

[22] Mining waste estimations in Albania include 12 million m^3 of chromium ores, 10 million tonnes or 6.5 million m^3 of copper ores, 4 million tonnes of nickel iron waste, 10 million tonnes of coal waste, and over 10 million tonnes of construction mineral waste, among others.

[23] The amended law forbids the production, import and sale of single-use plastic bags, including those that are defined as oxo-degradable or oxo-biodegradable. The legislation excludes those with a thickness of at least 70 microns that can hold a minimum of ten kilograms.

[24] In accordance with the law, the producer of specific waste streams is obliged to fulfill national objectives defined in the National Plan for Integrated Waste Management (2020-2035), which foresee a minimum of five functional EPR schemes by 2025 and a minimum of ten by 2030.

[25] Through the programme "Supporting Albanian Negotiation in Environment – Chapter 27 (SANE27) Phase II".

[26] The targets cover collection coverage, separate collection, landfilling rate, landfilling of biodegradable waste rate, recycling of construction and demolition waste, and recovery rate of packaging waste.

3 Selected priority areas of Albania's Circular Economy Roadmap

This chapter describes the selection process that led to the identification of three priority areas for Albania's Circular Economy Roadmap: economic instruments, circular business models for small and medium-sized enterprises, and the plastics life cycle with a focus on marine litter. It details the underlying consultation and decision-making processes and provides insights on the OECD methodology employed to determine these pertinent priority areas.

Approach taken to select the priority areas of the Roadmap

A key step to developing a national circular economy strategy or roadmap is to identify and select priority areas. The primary reason for such prioritisation is to help operationalise and ensure the focus of the circular economy roadmap. This is particularly important as the circular economy is a very broad concept, which encompasses actions across the entire economy as well as life cycle. The literature (Järvinen and Sinervo, 2020[1]; Ellen MacArthur Foundation, 2015[2]; Salvatori, Holstein and Böhme, 2019[3]) and the review of existing circular economy strategies and roadmaps that has been conducted in the context of previous OECD work show that there is no consensus on the definition of or approach to the selection of such focus areas. The review also showed that countries tend to focus only on a few priority sectors or areas, for example, on some key value chains, materials or horizontal areas where reforms would be the most impactful.

The review of international practices shows that countries have opted for customised quantitative and qualitative methodologies to inform their choice of specific priority areas. For Albania, the OECD proposed the approach described in Figure 3.1, which was also based on the availability of data and information.

Figure 3.1. Proposed approach for the selection of the priority areas of the Circular Economy Roadmap in Albania

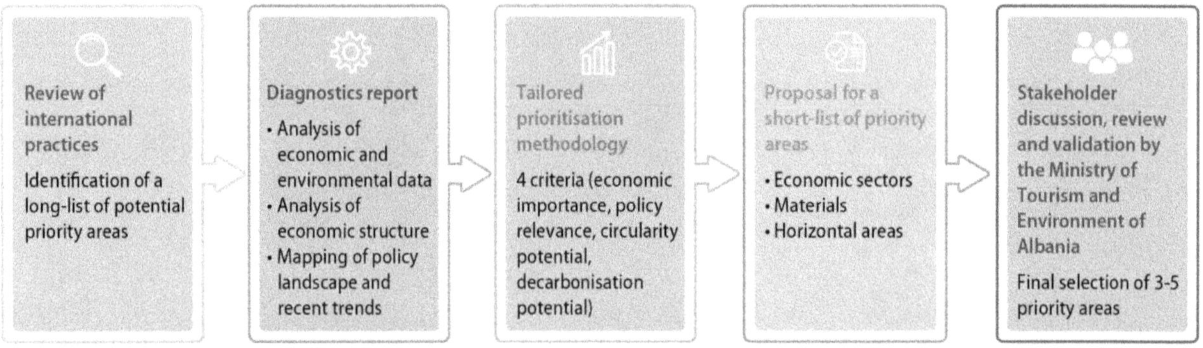

The tailored prioritisation methodology falls back on four criteria and their related indicators to inform the choice of (potential) priority areas:

- Economic importance, the assessment of which is largely data-driven. Relevant indicators include value added, employment and trade in sectors and industries, and the position of the sector in the global value chain.
- Policy relevance is assessed qualitatively by analysing whether a specific area has been included in relevant Albanian strategic documents and action plans, and to what extent, and whether a policy gap has been identified in the specific area. Since Albania is an EU candidate country on the path of aligning its regulatory framework with the EU *acquis*, the criterion also considers the policy relevance for the European Union, including whether there are specific EU targets and obligations in the considered area.
- Circularity potential can be assessed using a number of quantitative indicators, such as material productivity, material intensity, resource use, waste generation and recycling rates. Some of these indicators can be compared to an EU average or a specific target, which can provide insights on potential of specific areas to increase their circularity.
- Decarbonisation potential measured as the level of GHG emissions in specific sectors/industries, which can provide insights on sectors that offer the highest GHG emissions reduction potential. While decarbonisation is not a primary goal of a circular economy, it is an important benefit.

The diagnostics of the circular economy for Albania presented in Chapter 2 have been used as the primary source of data and information for the prioritisation exercise. As a result of this exercise, the OECD prepared a list of ten potential priority areas and their preliminary policy recommendations, presented and discussed at a stakeholder meeting in Albania. The working group was then asked to choose three to five priority areas from the proposed list.

Table 3.1 outlines the ten potential priority areas according to their level of priority (first, second and transversal) based on the four criteria discussed above (economic importance, policy relevance, circularity potential and decarbonisation potential). As the strict application of these four criteria was not feasible for horizontal or cross-cutting areas (e.g. economic instruments) that span various sectors and industries, additional indicators were used, such as the potential to achieve environmental outcomes, incentivise innovation, generate revenue, or provide incentives for consumers and businesses. This approach acknowledges the complexity and interconnectedness of sectors while ensuring a comprehensive assessment of different degrees of potential to contribute to decarbonisation and circularity.

Table 3.1. List of potential priority areas for the Circular Economy Roadmap in Albania

Proposed as the first priority	Proposed as the second priority	Proposed to be included transversally, across the chosen priority areas
Construction	Textile	Tourism
	Mining	
Biomass and food (agri-food system)	Plastics with a focus on marine litter	Municipal waste
Economic instruments	Circular business models for small and medium-sized enterprises	Awareness raising and education

Note: Areas shaded in grey correspond to horizontal areas that cut across sectors and materials.

Preliminary policy recommendations to illustrate all ten priority areas were proposed based on the diagnostics included in this document (see Chapter 2), additional desk research and stakeholder discussions, drawing on OECD expertise and previous work on the development of circular economy roadmaps.

The proposed policy recommendations are categorised into short, medium and long term. The emphasis in the short term (up to two years) is often on low-hanging fruit or measures that help to achieve a legal target/obligation, whereas the medium- (two to eight years) to long-term ones (eight years up to 2040) require certain foundations and prerequisites to be fulfilled. The approach also aims to encompass the entire value chain, from design and material sourcing to use and waste management.

Final selection of the priority areas

The three selected priority areas for the circular economy transition of Albania

Out of the ten identified potential priorities for the circular economy transition, Albania has chosen three priority areas for which the OECD provided more in-depth analysis and recommendations (details for each priority area are outlined in their respective chapters): 1) economic instruments; 2) circular business models for SMEs; and 3) plastics, with a focus on marine litter. Economic instruments and circular business models for SMEs are both cross-cutting areas, but while economic instruments focus on measures that change the behaviour of private actors through price signals, circular business models pay specific attention to providing an enabling framework for businesses. Plastics is a material-specific area, which covers measures to address (marine) plastic pollution throughout the life cycle.

Within the scope of the three selected priorities, stakeholders have emphasised the need for a specific focus on:

- Municipal waste management, which remains a major challenge in Albania, as more than 80% of waste is landfilled, recycling rates are low, the sector is heavily dependent on the informal waste sector and waste infrastructure is not functioning optimally.
- The tourism sector, on which Albania's economic growth is highly reliant. Given the recent growth of this industry, especially in coastal areas, which has caused environmental pressures, stakeholders considered it crucial to integrate circular economy principles into tourism. This would allow the destination to develop sustainably and generate a positive impact on the environment, local value chains and the labour market.
- Knowledge and awareness of the circular economy, which is generally limited in Albania, with authorities, enterprises and citizens alike often lacking an understanding of the opportunities and benefits that arise from a wider application of circular economy principles throughout society. This area has been identified as a key challenge that must be addressed in various sectors to facilitate a successful transition towards a circular economy.

Decision-making process

Stakeholder engagement played a key role in the development of this roadmap. Throughout the process, regular consultations with the circular economy working group (i.e. key circular economy stakeholders, including the government, private sector, civil society and academia) were held. Their views, experiences, challenges, needs and concerns regarding the circular transition were taken into consideration when developing diagnostics and they also informed the choice of priority areas (see Annex A).

Such consultations harbour the risk of some bias in the selection of the final priority areas. While the ten priority areas proposed were informed by indicators defined by the OECD, the final choice was the result of a decision-making process of the circular economy working group, endorsed by the Ministry of Tourism and Environment, the co-ordinating institution, responsible for the circular economy in Albania. While informed by OECD guidance, priority areas were thus selected in line with the Albanian government's economic and political agenda and the perspectives of a wide range of relevant stakeholders. This does not imply that some of the identified areas are considered irrelevant for Albania, but that they will not be the focus of this document. Instead, the diagnostics conducted by the OECD, included herein, provides a sound basis for the development and inclusion of other circular economy-related areas in relevant sector-focused strategies.

References

Ellen MacArthur Foundation (2015), *Delivering the Circular Economy: A Toolkit for Policymakers*, Ellen MacArthur Foundation, https://www.ellenmacarthurfoundation.org/a-toolkit-for-policymakers (accessed on 10 December 2020). [2]

Järvinen, L. and R. Sinervo (2020), *How to Create a National Circular Economy Road Map: A Guide to Making the Change Happen*, SITRA Studies No. 170, SITRA, Helsinki, https://www.sitra.fi/en/publications/how-to-create-a-national-circular-economy-road-map (accessed on 14 January 2021). [1]

Salvatori, G., F. Holstein and K. Böhme (2019), *Circular Economy Strategies and Roadmaps in Europe: Identifying Synergies and the Potential for Cooperation and Alliance Building – Study*, European Economic and Social Committee, Brussels, https://doi.org/10.2864/554946. [3]

4 Economic instruments

This chapter focuses on the "economic instruments" priority area, offering an analysis and suggesting policy recommendations to enhance circularity throughout the product value chain. Encompassing aspects related to product design, production, consumption patterns and end-of-life measures, the chapter examines existing policy instruments in Albania that could facilitate a transformative process, drawing insights from international best practices.

Definitions and concepts

Economic instruments are fiscal and other economic incentives and disincentives to incorporate environmental costs and benefits into the households' and enterprises' budgets. These can include subsidies, taxes, charges or fiscal transfers. The OECD defines economic instruments as "a means by which decisions or actions of government affect the behaviour of producers and consumers by causing changes in the prices to be paid for these activities" (OECD, 2008[1]).

Economic instruments have become an established and effective part of the waste management and circular economy policy landscape in OECD countries and beyond over the past four decades. Governments have used them to impact economic decisions throughout the life cycle (Figure 4.1). In contrast with regulation, these instruments seek to incentivise rather than compel private actors to take socially optimal decisions. They have two distinctive features: 1) they establish incentives for behaviour change; and 2) they offer flexibility in the degree and method to which actors can choose to change their behaviour. Ideally, incentives steer decisions towards a more circular pattern of activity, encouraging overall change and more vigorous innovation while leaving scope for cost-saving flexibility at the level of the individual decision maker.

Figure 4.1. Overview of economic instruments

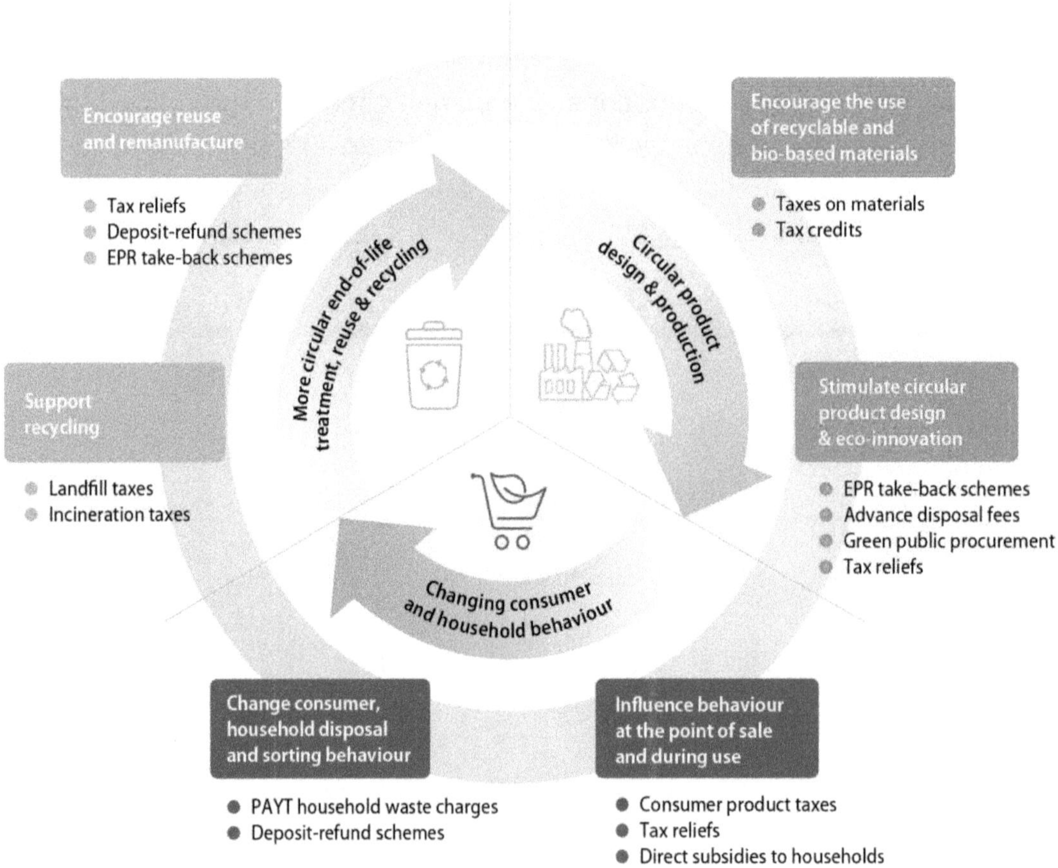

Note: EPR: extended producer responsibility; PAYT: pay-as-you-throw.
Source: Adapted from OECD (2022[2]).

Motivations for the selection of economic instruments as a key priority area of the Roadmap

Economic instruments offer the prospect of achieving desired environmental outcomes at a lower economic cost because they create continual incentives for behaviour change and innovation, while granting agents the autonomy to determine the extent of action they can manage or desire to pursue. Moreover, they can be potentially revenue-generating. Economic instruments have been a central part of environmental policy making and have helped implement countries' circular economy policies. In particular, there is a long history of economic instruments used to incentivise households to separate and properly dispose of waste as well as to drive increased recycling rates of municipal and industrial wastes. They are, therefore, an area with high policy relevance and circularity potential in Albania, as such measures will be essential for achieving its recycling reduction targets.

Economic instruments were selected as one of Albania's roadmap priorities as they can provide further impetus for reform, following the revision of key legislative and policy frameworks, in particular in the aforementioned area of waste management, but also public procurement. Beyond national policy, the inclusion of economic instruments in Albania is fundamental to meeting its goals under the Green Agenda for the Western Balkans as well as advancing its European Union (EU) accession process through further alignment with Chapter 27 of the EU acquis. The roadmap can be instrumental in charting a course for wider use of economic instruments in Albania and for them to drive the roadmap's successful implementation. In addition, the cross-cutting nature of this priority area provides a comprehensive and balanced approach to the country's transition to a circular economy, as it can accommodate a variety of economic instruments that are relevant for multiple economic sectors (including tourism) and materials and that provide economic incentives to private actors throughout the value chain.

Introducing economic instruments can support the decarbonisation of value chains across relevant economic sectors in Albania, such as two of the horizontal areas presented in this chapter: waste management and tourism. Mitigation actions in the waste sector are essential for Albania to achieve the targets set out in its latest Nationally Determined Contribution that would see an 18% reduction of greenhouse gas (GHG) emissions by 2030 in this sector compared to the 2016 baseline (Ministry of Tourism and Environment, 2022[3]). As a cross-sectoral industry, the direct decarbonisation potential of tourism is more difficult to quantify, though on a global level it is estimated to contribute around 5% of total GHG emissions (UNWTO and ITF, 2019[4]). Emissions in the tourism sector can mainly be attributed to international transport as well as other activities linked to retail trade, food services and accommodation.

Economic instruments can also help to unleash circularity potential in Albania, particularly through increasing recycling rates and incentivising the adoption of more sustainable tourism practices. Currently, a low 18% of municipal waste is recycled and recycling companies only operate at 25% of their production capacity. Tourism activities also show high circularity potential, as they are the largest contributors to domestic material consumption that is dominated by biomass (42%), mostly wood and food, and non-metallic minerals (40%) used for construction, a sector that has seen considerable growth through tourism.

Overview and approach to the selection of the proposed policy recommendations

As indicated above, this priority area pays specific attention to economic instruments that can improve municipal waste management, as municipal waste management has been identified as an area with very high policy relevance in Albania due to its link with several national and EU accession targets and obligations. With the revision of Albania's waste legislative framework to ensure alignment with the EU Waste Framework Directive and the well-defined objectives and targets for different waste streams in its two waste management strategies, municipal waste management is an area where economic instrument reforms can have the most impact. Economic instruments that can boost the sustainable development of other economic sectors – such as tourism, which has high policy and economic relevance for Albania – are also included in the recommendations.

Table 4.1 provides an overview of the proposed policy recommendations. They should be seen as a coherent policy package of economic instruments to achieve certain environmental outcomes rather than a list of individual economic instruments. Often a specific environmental goal requires a mix of instruments.

Table 4.1. Overview of the proposed policy recommendations in the economic instruments priority area for Albania

Short term	Medium term	Long term
Put in place planned extended producer responsibility take-back schemes	Implement landfill taxes with discounts for good sorting/high recycling	Introduce extended producer responsibility take-back schemes for new products (e.g. textiles)
Reform household waste charges (introduce a gradual increase of waste charges with discounts for good waste management practices, promote low-cost pay-as-you-throw schemes and improve enforcement)	Gradually increase the (mandatory) use of green criteria as award criteria in public procurement	Consider introducing material taxes on extracted materials/plastics
Introduce green public procurement, with a focus on priority sectors (capacity building, methodology guidelines)	Consider introducing a tourist tax to account for additional environmental costs related to tourism that are not covered by existing taxation schemes	Introduce minimum recycled content requirements within green public procurement (paper, plastics)
Introduce reuse and recycling credit schemes that offer payments for the removal of items from the municipal waste for recycling and reuse		Strengthen the use of tax relief for a circular economy (e.g. reduced value-added tax for eco-innovation, tax credits for food donations)
		Consider introducing incineration taxes

Key proposed policy recommendations

The proposed policy recommendations are structured around three key types of economic instruments:

1. extended producer responsibility (EPR) take-back schemes, which require firms to bear the costs of waste management for their post-consumer products, including responsibility for the collection and treatment of the products. In practice, EPR commits producers to take responsibility for collecting end-of-life products and for sorting them before their final treatment, ideally, recycling. This includes providing the financial resources to pay for the costs of related waste management and treatment activities.
2. fiscal instruments for the circular economy, which include environmental taxes and subsidies. In practice they work by changing the relative price of products and services. Environmental taxes impose a cost on firms and households for polluting activities, while subsidies decrease the cost of targeted products that have a positive impact on the environment. Subsidies indirectly increase the relative cost of polluting activities and products.
3. green public procurement (GPP) refers to public purchasing of products and services which are less environmentally damaging when taking into account their whole life cycle. GPP can provide industry incentives to innovate and develop environmentally friendly works, products and services with potentially lower waste disposal. They are also said to increase the supply of products and services that are more circular.

1. Increasing recycling and material recovery through EPR take-back schemes

EPR take-back schemes have been widely adopted by governments and companies and are currently the most commonly used for electronics, packaging, vehicles and tyres.

In Albania, municipal waste separation at source is almost non-existent, despite a legal obligation to do so. Only around 17% of generated municipal waste (for which estimates exist) is recycled (compared to 48% in the European Union) and the main method of managing municipal waste is disposal to landfill (80%) (INSTAT, 2023[5]; Eurostat, 2021[6]). A few pilot projects are, nevertheless, underway to introduce separate collection in some municipalities (in particular for paper and cardboard, aluminium, plastics, and bio-waste) and infrastructure is being improved with the construction of new recycling and incineration plants, mainly through funding from international development co-operation partners, with support provided through the EU4Circular Economy project. Moreover, a new law on EPR should be adopted in the second quarter of 2024 that will establish EPR take-back schemes for packaging; waste from electrical and electronic equipment; and batteries and accumulators in the country. The implementation of EPR schemes is planned as part of Albania's National Plan for Integrated Waste Management, with support also planned through the EU4Circular Economy project. Collected waste for which domestic recycling (or energy recovery) capacity does not exist can be exported for recovery operations under the international waste trade regime governed by a global environmental agreement, the Basel Convention on the Control of Transboundary Movements of Hazardous Wastes and their Disposal. The agreement covers hazardous and other wastes and has nearly universal membership with 191 Parties to date, including Albania (Basel Convention, n.d.[7]).

In the short term, Albania will need to put in place the planned EPR take-back schemes to shift end-of-life management costs of products from the public sector to producers and consumers and increase the collection and recycling rates of these waste streams (see also Chapter 6). To do so, Albania will first need to ensure the application of the following principles (the selection of principles is based on the OECD EPR Guidance (OECD, 2016[8])):

- Clear legal framework: The legislation needs to be clear on the definitions and responsibilities of all actors involved in EPR. There needs to be a legal framework for producer responsibility organisations (PROs) to operate. The EPR targets need to be periodically reviewed.
- Transparency: The governance of EPR systems needs to be transparent to provide more effective means for assessing the performance of the actors involved and holding them accountable for their activities. This will require collecting both technical and financial data and setting up registers of producers, accreditation of PROs and appropriate sanctions.
- Sufficient existing waste management capacity: For EPR systems to work effectively, adequate waste infrastructure needs to be in place across the country, including for waste separation at source, collection and treatment (ideally recycling).
- Administrative oversight capacity for better enforcement: This concerns enforcement capacity to prevent unauthorised facilities and collection points from operating. This should also minimise free-riding and non-compliance.
- Stakeholder engagement: Platforms for dialogue among stakeholders need to be established.

As underlined in the diagnostics (see Chapter 2), the current draft EPR Law in Albania largely covers aspects of the OECD EPR Guidance, such as clear rules on the creation and functioning of PROs, a defined governance structure, and co-ordination among responsible institutions for implementing the law, alongside the obligations (e.g. reporting) and sanctions against non-compliance of registered producers or PROs.

To facilitate the adoption of general good practices and OECD guidance on EPR, authorities and other actors covered by the new EPR Law in Albania could make use of the EPR Toolbox (PREVENT Waste Alliance, 2023[9]), to consult other international practices and participate in the knowledge exchange in order to enhance the functioning of the domestic EPR system. The EPR Toolbox contains three modules that span more general aspects of an EPR, including the monitoring of financial flows, but also focus on concrete actions, such as the integration of the informal sector or the creation of a market for recycled plastics (PREVENT Waste Alliance, 2023[9]). For example, as waste collection and sorting are labour-intensive, EPR schemes offer a great opportunity to integrate the informal waste sector into more formalised types of employment. PROs can offer attractive and formalised employment, thus encouraging waste collectors who have been working informally to apply for jobs (PREVENT Waste Alliance, 2023[9]).

Furthermore, it is important that Albania develops a system for proper data collection and processing. While certain technical requirements must be met, the first step towards ensuring the transparency of EPR schemes is effective co-ordination and compliance with reporting obligations under applicable legislation (namely, the EPR and the Law on Integrated Waste Management). The Czech Republic's electronic registry for waste is an exemplary model for a successful national waste information database. Recently rated as the best European system for waste data management and evaluation by the European Topic Centre for Circular Economy (Tuscano et al., 2022[10]), it employs two distinct systems. One handles the mandatory data reported by entities subject to relevant legal acts (Information System for Reporting Obligations) while the other manages the subsequent verification, processing and evaluation of the reported data (Information System for Waste Management). This streamlined process is further enhanced by extending verification authority to municipal and regional authorities, with the Environmental Information Agency functioning as the central data hub. By engaging a diverse array of stakeholders, including the statistical office, the information system becomes a catalyst for the development and implementation of evidence-based waste management policies.

In the long term, Albania can extend the EPR system to new product groups. This could include tyres (a common product group covered by EPR systems) and textiles. In particular, setting up an EPR scheme for textiles could be beneficial to manage the excess production of over 1 000 companies working in the sector in Albania. Moreover, it could also help Albania comply with the EU obligation to separately collect and achieve a high recycling rate of textiles by 2025. The European Commission has also proposed introducing mandatory and harmonised EPR rules for textiles as an amendment to the Waste Framework Directive, which would have to be transposed into the national legislation in all EU member states. Among EU countries, currently France and the Netherlands have a functioning EPR for textiles (Box 4.1 describes the example from France). Italy, Sweden and the United Kingdom are also considering implementing such a scheme.

Box 4.1. Extended producer responsibility for textiles and clothing in France

The extended producer responsibility (EPR) scheme for textiles (clothing, shoes and household linen) was introduced in France in 2007 under Article L-541-10-3 of the Environmental Code and further regulated by the enactment of the Anti-Waste and Circular Economy Law in 2020. It placed obligations on firms in the textiles and clothing sector in France to ensure a given standard of recovery and recycling. Firms could achieve this directly through their own actions or by contributing to an accredited producer responsibility organisation (PRO). In practice, a single non-profit PRO, Re_fashion (formerly Eco-TLC – Eco-organisme du textile, du linge et de la chaussure), has emerged as the sole vehicle for collective action in this sector. It was initiated in 2008 by a consortium of some 30 large retailers, manufacturers, wholesalers and industry organisations. In 2022, the PRO collected 260 kilotonnes from more than 6 500 marketers submitting declarations, comparable with the 827 kilotonnes of textiles placed on the market. While the collection rate increased by more than 15 000 tonnes compared to 2021, it remained below the national target (50% of products placed on the market).

Member contributions are based on the previous year's sales of items in four size categories of clothing and two categories of footwear. The contribution for a clothing item of average size was about EUR 1.16 cents in 2021. New eco-fees specifications are to be defined for the 2023-28 period. Reduced contribution rates ("eco-modulation") apply to producers promoting eco-design initiatives in three main areas: 1) durability; 2) the integration of recycled post-consumer materials; and 3) the introduction of recycled post-production materials. In 2021, the application of these reduced rates appears limited to less than 1.6% of total output, because the benefit of the reduced rates was insufficient to warrant the audit documentation that must be supplied. In 2022, the PRO carried out prospective studies for new eco-modulation criteria to address these challenges.

Re_fashion provides financial support for sorting and recycling facilities owned by private operators, including the non-profit organisations Le Relais and Emmaüs. Subject to meeting various performance and traceability requirements, a rate of 80 EUR/tonne is paid for items sent for reuse, 180 EUR/tonne for items sent to recycling and 20 EUR/tonne for items sent for energy recovery. Higher rates are paid to operators hiring disadvantaged workers. These subsidy payments account for about two-thirds of revenues from member contributions. Much of the remainder is devoted to consumer awareness campaigns and funding innovative demonstration projects and research.

In 2022, the reuse rate of collected textiles was roughly 59.5%. From its introduction in 2009 to 2022, the share of collected garments used as material for garnetting (recycling) grew from 14% to 31.3%; however, energy recovery also grew from 0% to 8.2%.

Sources: OECD (2022[11]); Re_fashion (2023[12]); Bukhari, Carrasco-Gallego and Ponce-Cueto (2018[13])

Two conditions could provide a good rationale for expanding EPR to certain product groups (OECD, forthcoming[14]):

1. A product group exhibits a relatively high cost of end-of-life management. This can be due to strict and costly requirements for the environmentally sound treatment of a specific end-of-life product or to the large waste volume and high share in overall waste.
2. There are opportunities for an EPR scheme to instigate changes in producer behaviour that lead to waste reduction, improved end-of-life handling or impact reduction during other phases of a product's life cycle.

2. Fiscal instruments for the circular economy

Environmental taxes and subsidies for increased reuse and recycling

In addition to the EPR take-back schemes, a number of fiscal instruments can change the waste disposal practices of those responsible for waste disposal towards more reuse and recycling. These typically include landfill and incineration taxes, which provide incentives to move up the waste hierarchy. There are also examples of countries that try to steer waste away from landfills by providing subsidies for redirecting waste destined for landfill to reuse or recycling. While fiscal instruments can provide cost certainty, their environmental impact depends on various factors, including the behavioural response from consumers and companies, a factor that is unknown *ex ante* (OECD, 2017[15]). The constant monitoring and adjustment of fiscal instruments must, therefore, be ensured to achieve the desired environmental outcome.

As indicated above, Albania currently faces many challenges in the area of waste management and does not implement any fiscal instruments that would divert waste away from landfills to operations such as reuse or recycling. Only around 89% of the population is covered by municipal waste services in Albania (INSTAT, 2021[16]), and the country still lacks adequate waste infrastructure, although international initiatives operating in Albania aim to address this challenge. Waste data monitoring also remains an important bottleneck to enforce proper waste management and implement waste-related taxes, as taxes tend to be based on quantities of disposed waste. While the waste reporting methodology was improved in 2021 and a project funded by international development co-operation partners supporting all municipalities in weighing their waste was conducted in 2022, waste data are still considered to be of poor quality. This is because they are primarily based on municipalities' and recycling companies' estimations, with the exception of the few municipalities that take their waste to a sanitary landfill or incinerator equipped with weighing equipment. Moreover, there is no systematic monitoring of the waste streams sent to dumpsites and no official data for industrial waste generated.

Certain pre-conditions, such as adequate waste treatment facilities, monitoring systems and a clear legal framework with rules and obligations for all actors involved, need to be put in place before such fiscal instruments can be effectively implemented. For example, to implement a landfill tax, it needs to be clear who pays the tax, on which waste and how much. Landfill taxes tend to be levied per tonne of waste, which requires that landfills be equipped with weighing equipment. Diverting waste away from landfill is possible only if alternative capacities for waste management exist across the country, municipal waste is properly collected from households and sorted at source or pre-treated before landfilling. Once the pre-conditions for a good functioning of waste-related taxes and subsidies are in place, Albania can take a number of actions to steer its waste towards reuse and recycling.

In the short term, Albania should consider introducing reuse and recycling credit schemes that would offer payments for the removal of items from the municipal waste for recycling and reuse. In Albania, most recyclable waste is still collected by informal waste pickers from dumpsites and bins and sold to the recycling industry. This is an illegal activity with potential health and environmental risks. To minimise these risks, Albania could set up a programme to facilitate the collection of recyclables from municipal waste through the use of third parties, who may be groups, charitable organisations or non-governmental organisations. The third parties would then be paid a credit or a subsidy per tonne of municipal waste collected and diverted from landfill to recycling. If this encourages employment in the informal sector through these third-party organisations, besides increased recycling, it may help also improve the socio-economic and environmental conditions pertaining to the activities of illegal waste pickers. Reuse and recycling credit schemes for local authorities as well as third parties are operating in the United Kingdom. These schemes are intended to incentivise the collection and recycling of municipal waste and could serve as an example of how to involve third parties in municipal waste management in Albania. Through these schemes, waste authorities pay credits to registered third parties (often non-governmental organisations) per tonne of reused or recycled waste that they collect from municipal waste destined for disposal. The size of the credit may correspond to the savings to the authority made by this reuse and recycling as they no longer need to pay the price for landfilling (North London Waste Authority, 2023[17]). Any programme aimed at diverting waste from landfill will require that landfilling has a cost. The cost of landfilling must be sufficiently high compared to recycling. The landfill cost can be increased by imposing a landfill tax on top of gate fees. To ensure that the majority of diverted waste is not redirected to incinerators, an incinerator tax could also be envisaged. Recent investments in waste incineration plants in Albania (the first one started operating in 2019 in Elbasan and two additional ones are being constructed in Fier and Tirana), as part of the government's plans to divert landfilling and close the estimated 199 large uncontrolled dumpsites by 2028, should not come at the expense of the recycling industry and should not diverge the country from aligning with the EU *acquis* waste hierarchy principle.

In this context, Albania will need to implement landfill taxes in the medium term and consider introducing incineration taxes in the long term to provide strong incentives for recycling. The landfill taxes will help divert waste away from landfilling while the incineration tax will ensure that this waste is not redirected to incinerators but rather to recycling. Many countries levy landfill taxes to reflect the environmental costs associated with landfill use. In the EU27, 23 EU member states have implemented a landfill tax, as have Switzerland and the United Kingdom, varying from 5 EUR/tonne (in Lithuania) to more than 100 EUR/tonne (in Belgium). Four EU member states do not have a landfill tax currently in place (Croatia, Cyprus,* Germany and Malta) (CEWEP, 2021[18]). These taxes are typically charged on the weight or volume of waste delivered to landfill sites or on the authorised landfill capacity. Landfill taxes have been implemented alone or in combination with landfill bans and incineration taxes/bans as well as other quantitative restrictions (e.g. Belgium, Denmark, Estonia, Finland and Sweden). The taxes need to be sufficiently high for them to be effective (or they need to be imposed with a high gate fee). A challenge for Albania may be that the industry and municipalities may not be able to pay a high price for landfilling, and recycling can be also costly (or not in place), which may give rise to illegal waste disposal and littering. To mitigate similar concerns, both the Czech Republic and the Slovak Republic have introduced gradually increasing landfill tax rates, which are differentiated per waste stream (for example, a higher tax for hazardous waste and recyclables and a lower tax for mixed municipal waste and inert waste). Moreover, the Slovak Republic has integrated a system of discounts and incentive subsidies for well-performing municipalities and industry stakeholders to decrease their landfill costs and motivate them to landfill less (Box 4.2). Other tax design elements relevant to consider include earmarking the proceeds from the collected landfill taxes to environmental funds and limiting the number of exemptions to the payment of this tax.

* Note by Türkiye: The information in this document with reference to "Cyprus" relates to the southern part of the Island. There is no single authority representing both Turkish and Greek Cypriot people on the Island. Türkiye recognises the Turkish Republic of Northern Cyprus (TRNC). Until a lasting and equitable solution is found within the context of the United Nations, Türkiye shall preserve its position concerning the "Cyprus issue".

Note by all the European Union Member States of the OECD and the European Union: The Republic of Cyprus is recognised by all members of the United Nations with the exception of Türkiye. The information in this document relates to the area under the effective control of the Government of the Republic of Cyprus.

Box 4.2. Landfill tax system in the Slovak Republic

Since 28 November 2018, the new Act No. 329/2018 Coll. on Landfill Taxes establishes that each person or entity depositing waste to landfill shall pay a landfill tax, even if the landfill site is located on their territory. The municipality pays for the municipal waste to be landfilled on behalf of households. The current landfill tax does not apply to waste used for construction works, sanitary works, reconstruction works or backfilling purposes. Government Decree No. 330/2018 Coll. sets the value of landfill taxes for the different waste streams and the distribution of the revenues from these taxes (the decree was amended in April 2022 to significantly increase the landfill tax rates for construction and demolition waste and industrial waste, in effect from July 2022). To landfill mixed municipal waste and bulky waste, the landfill tax is calculated based on the share of sorted municipal waste. The landfill tax for other waste is calculated based on the landfill tax applied to such waste and to its volume.

The municipality is obliged to publish the sorting rate of its municipal waste (kg separately collected waste/kg total municipal waste). The proceeds from the landfill tax are earmarked for the Environmental Fund, unlike previously, where the proceeds went directly to the municipalities in whose territory the landfill was located. The Slovak Environmental Fund will redistribute the proceeds to:

1. Municipalities in whose territory the landfills are located or through whose territory the roads to the landfill pass (as a form of compensation). In 2021, this was equivalent to 5 EUR/tonne of disposed non-hazardous waste and 33 EUR/tonne of disposed hazardous waste for municipalities with a landfill site.

The remaining tax proceeds are split as follows:

2. Municipalities which sort their municipal waste above a certain threshold (this could be seen as an incentive subsidy to sort better): 60% of the tax proceeds from landfilling municipal waste after the deduction of the contribution paid to the municipalities under point 1).
3. Municipalities which implement a separate collection for biodegradable kitchen waste from households and which recover all of this waste in a facility set up for this purpose (a form of incentive subsidy for food waste reduction): 15% of the tax proceeds from landfilling municipal waste + 15% of revenues from landfilling industrial waste after the deduction of the contribution to municipalities in point 1).
4. Waste management operators: 25% of the tax proceeds from landfilling municipal waste + 40% of the proceeds from landfilling industrial waste after the deduction of the contribution to municipalities under point 1).
5. Entities which demonstrate a lower production of waste in their production processes: 45% of the proceeds from landfilling industrial waste after the deduction of the contribution to municipalities under point 1).

According to Act No. 587/2004 Coll. on the Environmental Fund, which regulates the use of the revenues from the landfill tax, subsidies from such revenues can be used for activities in line with the goals set out in the Waste Prevention Programme and the Waste Management Plan of the Slovak Republic.

Source: OECD (2022[11]).

While there is no clear visible pattern to indicate that incineration taxes lead to higher recycling and lower landfilling and incineration rates (EEA, 2023[19]), this does not mean that incineration taxes have not been effective in diverting waste towards more recycling. Incineration taxes have been used in combination with other policy instruments that together as a policy package incentivise more recycling. They also help internalise the costs of negative externalities from GHG emissions associated with waste incineration and provide a clear signal to stakeholders that material recovery is to be prioritised over energy recovery. While energy recovery will help divert waste from landfills, to achieve the EU municipal waste recycling target of 65% and the landfill target of a maximum of 10% by 2035, only a relatively small share of municipal waste can be incinerated. Considering the contracts in place for the use of incinerators, Albania should ensure that it does not fall into a technological lock-in where overcapacity for energy recovery is created, which leads to fewer investments in recycling capacity.

Changing household disposal behaviour through municipal waste charges

Governments have introduced charges for the collection and disposal of household waste, which could be set as a flat fee, for example, per person per year, or as a fee based on the volume or weight of the waste collected, i.e. pay-as-you-throw (PAYT)-based charges. Different types of PAYT exist across countries and municipalities, which charge either directly, through individual measurement and billing (weight-based), or indirectly, through charges for bags, stickers or tokens, or by differentiating the charge by container size and the frequency of collection (volume-based). Several studies conclude that PAYT-based charges are more effective in inducing households to better sort their waste and increase municipal waste recycling rates compared to conventional flat-rate financed household waste collection charges (OECD, 2006[20]; Hogg, Sherrington and Vergunst, 2011[21]; Fullerton and Kinnaman, 1996[22]; EEA, 2016[23]).

Responsibility for household waste charges in Albania is a competency of municipalities, as they are responsible for municipal waste management. Currently, household waste charges in Albania are relatively low and insufficient to cover waste management costs. Moreover, municipalities struggle with enforcing the collection of waste charges. The European Environment Agency (EEA, 2021[24]) estimates that only around 20-40% of waste management costs are covered through these charges.

To strengthen the incentive effect of household waste charges on household behaviour, Albania will need to reform these charges, starting in the short term. The government will need to consider the potential redistribution impacts, as the increased price of waste collection may disproportionately impact low-income households. Therefore, it is proposed that the reform include the following elements:

- Gradual increase of household waste charges but with discounts for good waste management practices. For example, Italy introduced a discount for households on their waste charges if the household does home composting (Box 4.3). Some municipalities in the Slovak Republic (e.g. Bratislava) subsidised the cost of the starting kit (caddies and biodegradable bags) for separate collection of bio-waste for its residents to support the introduction of bio-waste collection in the city. These measures could be particularly relevant in Albania, as around 60% of waste generated is organic and three composting plants have recently started operating, with five additional plants planned to be opened in the short term (INSTAT, 2021[16]).
- Promotion of the implementation of low-cost PAYT schemes. Municipalities may choose the type of PAYT scheme that will work best for them, also given the existing waste management infrastructure, weighting equipment and costs. Typically, volume- and frequency-based schemes (including sack-based schemes)[1] tend to be less expensive to set up and operate than weight-based schemes; however, the weight-based schemes appear to be more effective in reducing the amount of household waste (Hogg, Sherrington and Vergunst, 2011[21]; OECD, 2006[20]). A hybrid system of individual billing based on a flat fee plus a variable charge could be also promoted, as a number of foreign municipalities (e.g. Parma in Italy) have done (Box 4.3).
- Households should only pay for the collection of their mixed waste and waste streams not covered by an EPR take-back scheme. As EPR systems are more widely implemented in Albania, the costs of the collection of recyclables should be financed more extensively by producers.
- Different solutions may need to apply to rural and urban areas. The waste collection and treatment infrastructure is likely to differ across the country depending on the population density of the different areas. In more densely populated areas with multi-family apartment buildings, which are

more common in urban areas, kerbside collection might be more cost-effective and more frequent than in areas with a low population density living in single-family homes. Volume frequency-based PAYT schemes may also be easier to implement in more densely populated apartment blocks than weight-based or bag systems, but their effectiveness in reducing mixed waste might be lower (as the incentive to reduce waste for individual households is more diluted in multi-family apartment buildings than in single-family homes where the discarded waste can be directly attributed to the household). In less densely populated areas, pay-per-bag charges have been set up in Bergamo (Italy), for example. The system in Bergamo functions based on compulsory purchasing of special bags for residual waste using a smart card associated to each household. Over time, the scheme helped increase the separate collection levels in the province of Bergamo to 57% (up from 42.5%) (Province of Bergamo, 2020[25]).

- A comprehensive awareness- and knowledge-raising campaign is critical to secure public acceptance of increased environmental charges, such as for municipal waste services. A higher financial burden and potentially regressive effects on income must be well communicated to avoid resistance from consumers while considering the introduction of compensatory measures for lower income households (Vona, 2021[26]). Higher revenues should also be justified for concrete uses in improved waste management that would result in tangible benefits for paying customers (i.e. a cleaner, immediate environment and improved health), to promote their participation.

Box 4.3. Examples of positive incentives within household waste charges from Italy

Waste charges consisting of a flat fee and a variable pay-as-you-throw based fee

In Parma, the waste fee is composed of two main elements: 1) a fixed part based on the number of household members and the square metres of the household; and 2) a variable part that essentially depends on residual waste generation (accounted in terms of number of set-outs) and home composting. The fixed part covers a minimum number of collections of residual waste per household, which is intended to cover the fixed costs of managing the system and concurrently to prevent dumping and littering. Additional removals are charged (EUR 0.7 per bag, EUR 1.4 per bucket and EUR 4.2 per wheeled bin). In terms of positive incentives, households get a 12% reduction in their fee if they do home composting. Households using nappies are not charged for the extra removals.

Similarly, in Contarina, the fee is composed of a flat and a variable fee. The variable fee penalises the number of times the non-recyclable dry waste bin is emptied and provides a bonus for those households doing home composting equal to a 30% reduction of the variable fee.

Sources: OECD (2022[11]); Zero Waste Europe (2018[27]); Zero Waste Europe (2018[28])

Experience from other EU member states demonstrates that a policy mix of measures is needed to support the implementation of household waste charges that would provide incentives for behaviour change, such as the implementation of well-designed PAYT schemes. This includes the introduction of additional economic instruments, such as landfill taxes and EPR programmes, as well as awareness raising on waste sorting and separate collection to counteract public misconception and opposition. Moreover, adequate and convenient waste infrastructure for waste separation and collection is also a pre-condition for a well-functioning municipal waste management system as well as a supporting regulatory framework (e.g. landfill bans, enforcement).

Environmental tourist tax for managing the external environmental costs of tourism

Albania has a strong tourism sector, which may generate negative environmental impacts that are not accounted for by existing economic instruments. Despite Albania's rich natural and cultural heritage, the current growth of the industry is spurred mainly by mass short-stay and low-cost beach tourism during the summer months. Moreover, the expansion of the sector is often at odds with environmental goals. Significant and timely investments will be necessary to ensure a more responsible development of tourism through diversified activities, resilient infrastructure, specialised accommodations and quality jobs that respect the local environmental and social context. To this end, increased total tax revenue by the tourism sector could be earmarked for compensating the negative environmental impacts of tourism.

To help internalise the external environmental cost of tourism activities that are not accounted for by existing taxes or levies, Albania may consider introducing an environmental tax on tourism in the medium term. This tax may have differentiated rates depending on the environmental impact associated with different types of tourism. This could promote a change of preference in terms of tourism activities and/or compensate for the costs associated with tourism. However, as tourism affects different environmental fields (water, energy, mobility, waste, etc.), such a tax should not merely focus on promoting a circular economy and waste management and may be better suited to address a combination of different environmental externalities (OECD, 2023[29]).

Several European countries have implemented tourist taxes at the regional, local or city level (e.g. Switzerland, Amsterdam, Catalonia, Lisbon); however, in most cases, these are not environmental taxes, as their main goal is generating revenue rather than achieving some environmental performance goals. Typically, these taxes are fixed charges per night ranging from EUR 0.50 to EUR 5 or charged as a percentage of the price of the accommodation (up to 7% in Amsterdam). In Albania, municipalities can set a tax up to 5% of the accommodation price per night (Ministry of Finance and Economy, n.d.[30]). In the municipality of Tirana, for example, this varies between accommodation types, ranging from around EUR 1-3 per night, but not all municipalities make use of a tourist tax. While several tourist taxes use revenues to relieve some of the (environmental) pressures caused by tourism, there are few cases in Europe where the tax rate itself varies with explicit environmental criteria (e.g. the Balearic Islands Tourist Tax) (OECD, 2023[29]).

Based on these examples, there are a few aspects to take into consideration when considering an environmental tax on tourism (OECD, 2023[29]):

- Fiscal exemptions and preferential treatment in existing taxes or levies granted to the tourism sector and related to environmental externalities should be removed. For example, the tourism sector should not be taxed at lower rates for water consumption or municipal waste than residents.
- The tax could account for the costs of constructing and maintaining additional infrastructure capacity, such as roads, housing, water systems, and sewage pipes and waste services, which is only used during tourism peaks and that is typically paid for by local residents.

Environmental taxes for the uptake of secondary raw materials by producers

In the long term, Albania could explore the option of introducing new taxes on materials, such as construction aggregates or non-recyclable plastics, to increase the use of secondary or alternative materials. This would be particularly relevant in Albania with the recent growth of the construction sector, spurred by significant infrastructure and residential development. Albania could consider introducing a tax on aggregates, such as stones, gravel or sand, to send a strong price signal that would effectively diminish the attractiveness of sourcing in the mining and quarrying industry as well as the later use of such virgin materials for construction. Moreover, following the example of many EU member states (EEA, 2008[31]), resource charges could be considered for mining and extractions to cover the substantial administrative costs of reviewing environmental impact assessments and monitoring permit compliance. Empirical evidence from Denmark, Sweden and the United Kingdom suggests that imposed taxes on aggregates have contributed to a reduction in the use of primary aggregates in these countries in spite of their relatively low price elasticity.[2] However, the experience also suggests that additional policies, such as quality standards and subsidies, are needed to increase the demand for and supply of recycled and secondary aggregates (Söderholm, 2011[32]; EEA, 2008[31]). These taxes should be distinguished from royalty payments that are associated with resource extraction. Unlike environmental taxes on aggregates aimed at increasing the use of secondary raw materials, resource royalties are only collected for revenue and social redistribution purposes (Otto et al., 2006[33]). Both instruments aim to address environmental and natural resource management issues; however, they serve distinct purposes and are applied differently in practice. Environmental taxes focus on internalising the costs of extractive activities and associated pollution while royalties are payments made for the use of virgin resources, ensuring equitable compensation among stakeholders involved in the extraction process (e.g. government, landowners, companies). Combined they offer a comprehensive approach to sustainable resource management, balancing economic incentives with environmental protection and equitable distribution of benefits.

Taxes on plastics intended to encourage the incorporation of secondary material in the design of products have been less widely used so far than taxes on single-use plastic items (e.g. plastic bags). While Albania amended its Waste Management Law to ban the use of certain categories of plastic bags in March 2022, there is currently no tax on certain plastic materials, such as non-recyclable plastic packaging. Such a tax could support the uptake of recycled plastic across a wide range of plastic packaging products, therefore, helping to reduce the consumption of virgin plastics (see Chapter 6).

Use of subsidies to support waste reduction

Countries also employ a diversity of tax benefits to stimulate upstream circular production strategies to use more recycled materials or upcycled products and support R&D and eco-innovation in general, including technologies and processes that eliminate or reduce waste throughout the production process. Most tax benefits, such as tax deductions from the corporate income tax, accelerated depreciation schemes and reduced/exempt value-added tax (VAT) rates are not circular economy-specific but apply to environmental investments.

Several countries also use tax benefits, such as exempt or reduced VAT rates or tax credits for food donations. Although the primary objective of food donation is not food waste reduction but to ensure the availability of good and healthy food to people from vulnerable groups, the potential to divert unsold products to these end-consumers does coincide with food waste prevention goals.

Albania does not have a legal and regulatory framework for encouraging food donations by local businesses to food banks (Food Bank Albania, 2023[34]).

In the long term, Albania could consider introducing new tax relief in the form of reduced or exempted VAT rates or tax credits that would support waste reduction objectives. This can be achieved directly, for example, by implementing tax credits or reduced/exempted VAT for food donations that help achieve food waste reduction in the food industry. Such a system would also require a clear legal framework with assigned responsibilities and rules on which food can be donated, as well as an infrastructure of food banks that would distribute donated food to vulnerable groups. Support for waste reduction objectives can also be achieved indirectly through broader tax relief for broader environmental investments. Such instruments should be implemented as part of a wider policy mix, where additional policy measures would help direct innovations to those that help reduce waste, such as eco-design requirements and promoting waste prevention through targeted communication and information tools.

3. Green public procurement for a more circular supply of products and services

GPP incentivises service providers to supply and invest in products and services that are more circular through the purchasing power of public authorities, which can be substantial in certain areas, such as infrastructure.

In Albania, the current Public Procurement Law (2020) prescribes contracting authorities to respect the requirements of environmental, social and labour legislation. The law further provides for the possibility of including environmental and climate impacts in the award criteria (OECD, 2022[35]). In terms of policies, Albania adopted its first comprehensive National Public Procurement Strategy (2020-2023) in November 2020. It includes actions directed at developing specific legal provisions for the Public Procurement Law or secondary legislation for GPP, but no concrete advancements have been reported to date (Public Procurement Agency of Albania, 2023[36]). The Public Procurement Agency published a Green Procurement Roadmap (outlining rules for voluntary implementation) and a methodology related to GPP (providing general instructions and guidance on minimum requirements) in 2023 (Public Procurement Agency of Albania, 2023[37]). There is currently no information on the revision of the National Public Procurement Strategy (2020-2023).

To benefit from public authorities' purchasing power to increase the supply of circular products and services, Albania will need to establish an effective GPP system.

In the short term, Albania will need to ensure that a national GPP strategy and action plan include green criteria and targets for selected product groups, supported by sector- or product-specific methodological guidelines and capacity-building programmes for public authorities as well as other stakeholders. The most common product groups for which GPP criteria tend to be applied include copy and graphic paper, office IT equipment, food and catering services, or construction works. Addressing the specific needs of Albania's construction sector within this framework might be particularly impactful, given the levels of emissions[3] and public expenditure associated with this sector. There is a vast opportunity for Albania to reduce the environmental impact of public infrastructure projects, including tourist accommodation, by adopting GPP guidelines, criteria and targets for more circular and sustainable construction works.

In the medium term, Albania may want to gradually increase the use of green criteria among public authorities, in particular as award criteria. This can be done through stronger promotion of GPP among public authorities at all levels of government, developing a catalogue of good practices that potential suppliers may consult or introducing a mandatory element into the GPP. For example, the Slovak Republic has a mandatory application of GPP criteria in place for four product groups for state-level public entities. In 2022, the Slovak Public Procurement Act was amended to oblige state-level entities to include environmental aspects in public procurement in at least 6% of annual contracts (OECD, 2022[11]). There is no evidence of mandatory GPP criteria being more effective than voluntary ones, as the actual impact depends on the type of green criteria applied. These may be basic, and hence easy to comply with, with a small environmental benefit as a result (for example, a requirement to implement an ISO standard). When taking the mandatory approach, attention must be paid to ensure that sufficient incentives are still in place for bidders to compete on green criteria rather than solely on price (once the minimum environmental criteria are fulfilled) and that the pool of potential bidders does not become too restricted by applying overly strict selection criteria.

In the long term, Albania may use this economic instrument to support the use of secondary raw materials by introducing minimum recycled content requirements within GPP. This may be focused on paper and plastics materials in product groups, such as copy and graphic paper, and office supplies and furniture. In particular, focusing on plastics would also support the implementation of measures outlined in the plastics priority area. Box 4.4 provides an example of introducing minimum recycled content requirements from Italy and Japan.

Box 4.4. Examples of introducing minimum recycled content requirements within green public procurement

Japan

The Japanese Act on Promoting Green Procurement and its related Basic Policy on Green Procurement specifies environmental criteria to be considered when purchasing goods and services by the government or its administrative agencies. The environmental criteria include, among others, recycled content criteria for pulp and plastics used in the products designated for procurement. For example, the higher the recycled content share in an evaluated good, the higher the evaluation score for that good. For some of the goods, the policy requires minimum recycled content requirements. This is the case, for example, for coated inkjet colour printer paper, where at least 70% recycled pulp content is required, or for stationery products where items containing plastics contain at least 40% recycled plastics in weight of the total plastics and items containing paper contain at least 50% recycled pulp. Green public procurement (GPP) is mandatory for government agencies across a wide array of product categories.

Italy

Since 2016, all public entities in Italy are obliged to apply GPP criteria for products and services for which GPP criteria have been defined (Italian Public Contract Code). For some products, the presence of recycled content constitutes an award criterion that improves the evaluation score for the good or service. This is the case, for instance, of GPP criteria for textile products that reward the presence of recycled textile fibres or of by-products from industrial symbiosis processes as well as goods prepared for reuse and the presence of additional repair and maintenance services offered for the goods supplied (Ministerial Decree 30/06/21). Specific voluntary labelling and certification schemes enable companies to declare compliance with GPP criteria (both minimum and award criteria), such as the Remade in Italy environmental certification for recycled content. Moreover, minimum recycled content requirements constitute eligibility criteria to benefit from certain tax benefits targeted at enterprises.

Source: OECD (2024[38]); Ministry of the Environment, Japan (2000[39])

References

Basel Convention (n.d.), *Basel Convention – Overview*, https://www.basel.int/theconvention/overview/tabid/1271/default.aspx. [7]

Bukhari, M., R. Carrasco-Gallego and E. Ponce-Cueto (2018), “Developing a national programme for textiles and clothing recovery”, *Waste Management & Research: The Journal for a Sustainable Circular Economy*, Vol. 36/4, pp. 321-331, https://doi.org/10.1177/0734242x18759190. [13]

CEWEP (2021), *Landfill Taxes and Restrictions*, Consideration of European Waste-to-Energy Plants, Brussels, https://www.cewep.eu/wp-content/uploads/2021/10/Landfill-taxes-and-restrictions-overview.pdf. [18]

Climate Watch (2022), *Data Explorer - Historical Emissions*, https://www.climatewatchdata.org/data-explorer/historical-emissions (accessed on 23 November 2023). [40]

EEA (2023), *Economic Instruments and Separate Collection Systems: Key Strategies to Increase Recycling*, European Environment Agency, Copenhagen, https://www.eea.europa.eu/publications/economic-instruments-and-separate-collection. [19]

EEA (2021), *Municipal Waste Management in Western Balkan Countries: Albania*, European Environment Agency, Copenhagen, https://www.eea.europa.eu/themes/waste/waste-management/municipal-waste-management-country/albania-municipal-waste-factsheet-2021/#:~:text=Albania%20has%20a%20new%20national,the%20treatment%20of%20residual%20MSW. [24]

EEA (2016), *Municipal Waste Management Across European Countries*, European Environment Agency, Copenhagen, https://www.eea.europa.eu/publications/municipal-waste-management-across-european-countries. [23]

EEA (2008), *Effectiveness of Environmental Taxes and Charges for Managing Sand, Gravel and Rock Extraction in Selected EU Countries*, EEA Report No. 2/2008, European Environment Agency, Copenhagen, https://www.eea.europa.eu/publications/eea_report_2008_2 (accessed on 22 November 2023). [31]

Eurostat (2021), "Municipal waste statistics", https://ec.europa.eu/eurostat/databrowser/view/env_wasmun/default/table?lang=en (accessed on 6 December 2023). [6]

Food Bank Albania (2023), *Annual Report 2022*, Food Bank Albania, https://foodbank.al/wp-content/uploads/FBA-Annual-Report-2022-v5-EMAIL.pdf. [34]

Fullerton, D. and T. Kinnaman (1996), "Household responses to pricing garbage by the bag", *The American Economic Review*, Vol. 86/4, pp. 971-984, http://www.jstor.org/stable/2118314. [22]

Hogg, D., C. Sherrington and T. Vergunst (2011), *A Comparative Study on Economic Instruments Promoting Waste Prevention: Final Report to Bruxelles Environnement*, Eunomia, Bristol, United Kingdom, https://document.environnement.brussels/opac_css/elecfile/Etude%20dechets%20Eunomia%20Report%20en (accessed on 22 July 2021). [21]

INSTAT (2023), "Urban waste in tonnes by urban waste treatment, type and year", http://databaza.instat.gov.al/pxweb/en/DST/START__EN__MU/MU05 (accessed on 2 November 2023). [5]

INSTAT (2021), *Urban Solid Waste*, Institute of Statistics, Tirana, https://www.instat.gov.al/media/10524/urban-solid-waste-2021__.pdf. [16]

Ministry of Finance and Economy (n.d.), "Hotel accomodation tax", web page, https://financa.gov.al/taksa-e-fjetjes-ne-hotel. [30]

Ministry of the Environment, Japan (2000), *Act on Promotion of Procurement of Eco-Friendly Goods and Services by the State and Other Entities (Act on Promoting Green Procurement)*, Government of Japan, https://www.env.go.jp/en/laws/policy/green/index.html (accessed on 4 November 2021). [39]

Ministry of Tourism and Environment (2022), *The Fourth National Communication of Albania on Climate Change*, Ministry of Tourism and Environment, Tirana, https://unfccc.int/sites/default/files/resource/Fourth%20National%20Communication%20of%20Albania%20to%20the%20UNFCCC_EN.pdf. [3]

North London Waste Authority (2023), "Reuse and recycling credits scheme", web page, https://www.nlwa.gov.uk/article/reuse-and-recycling-credits-scheme (accessed on 15 November 2023). [17]

OECD (2024), *Material consumption* (indicator), https://doi.org/10.1787/84971620-en (accessed on 20 February 2024). [38]

OECD (2023), *Environmental Tax Policy Review of Andalusia*, OECD Publishing, Paris, https://doi.org/10.1787/fe6d8b45-en. [29]

OECD (2022), *Closing the Loop in the Slovak Republic: A Roadmap Towards Circularity for Competitiveness, Eco-innovation and Sustainability – Annexes*, OECD, Paris, https://www.oecd.org/env/waste/Closing-the-Loop-in-the-Slovak-Republic-Annexes.pdf. [11]

OECD (2022), "Closing the loop in the Slovak Republic: A roadmap towards circularity for competitiveness, eco-innovation and sustainability", *OECD Environment Policy Papers*, No. 30, OECD Publishing, Paris, https://doi.org/10.1787/acadd43a-en. [2]

OECD (2022), *SME Policy Index: Western Balkans and Turkey 2022: Assessing the Implementation of the Small Business Act for Europe*, SME Policy Index, OECD Publishing, Paris, https://doi.org/10.1787/b47d15f0-en. [35]

OECD (2017), "Environmental fiscal reform: Progress, prospects and pitfalls (archived)", OECD, Paris, https://www.oecd.org/tax/tax-policy/environmental-fiscal-reform-G7-environment-ministerial-meeting-june-2017.pdf. [15]

OECD (2016), *Extended Producer Responsibility: Updated Guidance for Efficient Waste Management*, OECD Publishing, Paris, https://doi.org/10.1787/9789264256385-en. [8]

OECD (2008), *OECD Glossary of Statistical Terms*, OECD Publishing, Paris, https://doi.org/10.1787/9789264055087-en. [1]

OECD (2006), "Impacts of unit-based waste collection charges", *OECD Papers*, OECD Publishing, Paris, https://doi.org/10.1787/oecd_papers-v6-art30-en. [20]

OECD (forthcoming), *New Aspects of EPR: Extending Producer Responsibility to Additional Product Groups and Challenges Throughout the Product Lifecycle*, OECD, Paris, forthcoming. [14]

Otto, J. et al. (2006), *Mining Royalties: A Global Study of Their Impact on Investors, Government, and Civil Society*, World Bank, Washington, DC, https://doi.org/10.1596/978-0-8213-6502-1. [33]

PREVENT Waste Alliance (2023), *EPR Toolbox*, GIZ, Bonn, Germany, https://prevent-waste.net/epr-toolbox. [9]

Province of Bergamo (2020), "Waste observatory", https://www.provincia.bergamo.it (accessed on 25 January 2020). [25]

Public Procurement Agency of Albania (2023), *GPP Roadmap*, Public Procurement Agency of Albania, Tirana, https://www.app.gov.al/legislation/public-procurement/roadmap. [37]

Public Procurement Agency of Albania (2023), *National Procurement Strategy 2020-2023: Monitoring Report January to December 2022*, Public Procurement Agency of Albania, Tirana, https://www.app.gov.al/GetData/DownloadDoc?documentId=515f9cb3-c71d-496c-a9cc-48ef56b6f735. [36]

Re_fashion (2023), *2022 Activity Report*, Re_fashion, https://refashion.fr/rapport-activite/2022/en/#page/1. [12]

Söderholm, P. (2011), "Taxing virgin natural resources: Lessons from aggregates taxation in Europe", *Resources, Conservation and Recycling*, Vol. 55/11, pp. 911-922, https://doi.org/10.1016/j.resconrec.2011.05.011. [32]

Tuscano, J. et al. (2022), *Electronic Registries for Waste Across Europe*, ETC CE Report 2022/3, European Topic Centre for Circular Economy and Resource Use, https://www.eionet.europa.eu/etcs/etc-ce/products/etc-ce-products/etc-ce-report-3-2022-electronic-registries-for-waste-across-europe (accessed on 22 November 2023). [10]

UNWTO and ITF (2019), *Transport-related CO2 Emissions of the Tourism Sector: Modelling Results*, United Nations World Tourism Organization, Madrid, https://doi.org/10.18111/9789284416660. [4]

Vona, F. (2021), "Managing the distributional effects of environmental and climate policies: The narrow path for a triple dividend", *OECD Environment Working Papers*, No. 188, OECD Publishing, Paris, https://doi.org/10.1787/361126bd-en. [26]

Zero Waste Europe (2018), *The Story of Contarina: Case Study #4*, Zero Waste Europe, https://zerowasteeurope.eu/wp-content/uploads/2019/10/zero_waste_europe_cs4_contarina_en.pdf. [28]

Zero Waste Europe (2018), *The Story of Parma: Case Study #7*, Zero Waste Europe, https://zerowasteeurope.eu/wp-content/uploads/2019/10/zero_waste_europe_cs7_parma_en.pdf. [27]

Notes

[1] In a volume-based PAYT scheme, households are charged based on the volume or size of the waste they generate. This could be measured by the capacity of the waste container or the number of bags of waste generated. Frequency-based PAYT schemes charge households based on the frequency of waste collection. This could involve a fixed fee for each collection or a subscription model where households pay for a certain number of collections per month or year. Sack-based PAYT schemes involve households using designated waste sacks or bags provided by the waste management authority. The cost is associated with the purchase of these sacks, and households are charged based on the number of sacks they use. This method encourages waste reduction, as households are mindful of the amount of waste they dispose of in the designated sacks.

[2] As the cost of aggregates is low in relation to overall construction costs, demand for aggregates is generally considered price inelastic.

[3] The manufacturing and construction sector contributed 12% of total GHG emissions in Albania in 2020, in third place after agriculture, transport and industry in terms of total contribution to GHG emissions (Climate Watch, 2022[40]). Most of the emissions in this sector can be attributed to the use of carbon-intensive material, largely cement. Estimates for this sector vary across sources due to the use of different methodologies.

5 Circular business models for small and medium-sized enterprises

This chapter outlines policy recommendations aimed at promoting the transition to circular business models in the Albanian economy, specifically focusing on small and medium-sized enterprises. It presents the state-of-play and existing policy framework, points out potential areas for improvement, and proposes a set of specific policy recommendations that draw inspiration from relevant international good practices.

What are circular business models?

Circular business models represent fundamentally different ways of producing and consuming goods and services than the traditional linear business models. They aim to reduce the extraction and use of materials, minimise waste generation, and use existing materials and products as inputs to production through reuse and recycling. By doing so, they help reduce the negative environmental impacts of material consumption.

Circular business models can be classified into five main types (Figure 5.1) (OECD, 2019[1])

1. **Circular supply models** involve the replacement of traditional production inputs with bio-based, renewable or recovered materials. By doing so, they reduce the demand for virgin materials in the long run. These models target the design phase of production and sourcing of materials.
2. **Resource recovery models** involve the production of secondary raw materials from waste streams. They thereby divert waste from final disposal and reduce the extraction and processing of virgin materials. There are three main components for the model to work: 1) waste collection; 2) sorting; and 3) the production of secondary materials from waste.
3. **Product life extension models** involve extending the lifetime of products. This can be achieved by designing products in a way that increases their durability, by reuse and repair activities and remanufacturing.
4. **Sharing models** facilitate the sharing of underutilised products through, for example, online platforms, through co-ownership or co-access. This can reduce demand for new products and materials.
5. **Product service systems models** involve selling services rather than products. Since the service provider remains the owner of the product that provides the "service", this increases incentives for circular product design that increases durability and reparability as well as more efficient product use.

The distinction between the different types of circular business models is less clear-cut in reality, as in some cases businesses adopt a combination of these models.

Figure 5.1. Typology of circular business models

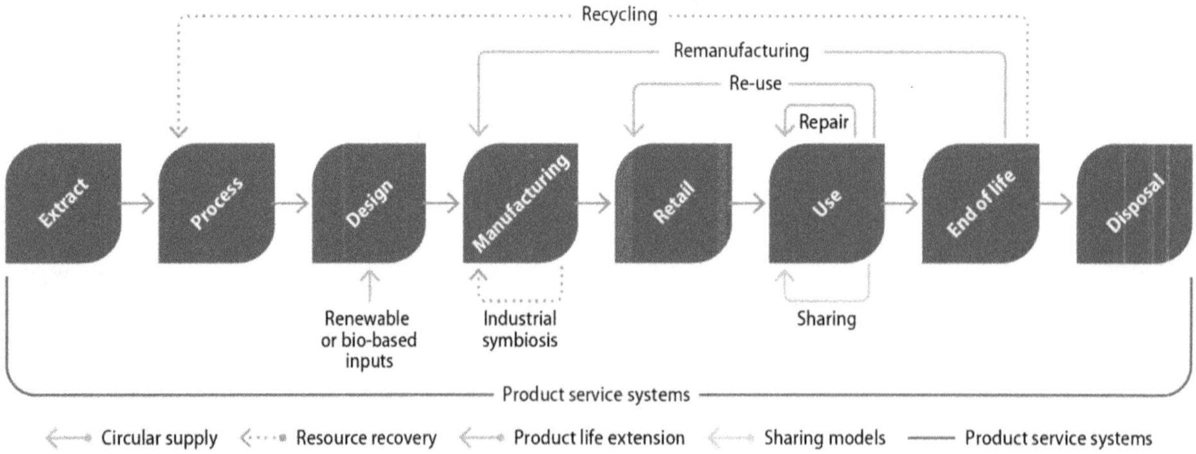

Source: Adapted from Lacy and Rutqvist (2015[2]).

Motivation for the selection of circular business models with a focus on small and medium-sized enterprises as a key priority area of the Roadmap

Circular business models for small and medium-sized enterprises (SMEs) have been selected because of their high economic importance, high policy relevance, high circularity potential and possibly important decarbonisation potential for Albania. SMEs are the backbone of the Albanian economy, accounting for 99.8% of enterprises and 81.9% of employment; 85% of them work in services (OECD, 2022[3]). Albania also implements a number of policies that target and support SMEs, for example, its newest SME strategy, the Business Development and Investment Strategy (2021-2027) (Government of Albania, 2021[4]), includes environmental policies targeting SMEs which aims to boost the circular economy and eco-innovation. Since SMEs, on aggregate, have a significant environmental footprint (small firms account for 50% of greenhouse gas [GHG] emissions in the world (ICT, 2021[5])), it is essential that Albania considers them in its environmental policy making. Moreover, on the one hand, like any other economic entity, SMEs face the consequences of environmental degradation, which can generate specific challenges for their survival and growth. On the other hand, and more importantly, they can be a source of innovation and solutions to develop the technologies needed to address these environmental challenges. Circular business models, like economic instruments, can also help decarbonise GHG-intensive activities related to waste management and tourism by tapping into the circular opportunities in these areas (see section "Motivations for selecting economic instruments as a key priority area of Albania's Circular Economy Roadmap" in Chapter 4). New green markets, such as the circular economy, can also create new business opportunities for SMEs. Even without moving into new markets, SMEs can potentially improve the performance of their business by realising efficiency gains and cost reductions by greening their products, services and processes. In this regard, tailored policies, incentives and instruments are necessary to enable them to participate in the green transition, as SMEs face a number of barriers (financial, informational, etc.) in their greening efforts, and more so than large firms (OECD, 2021[6]).

Different types of circular business models (see Figure 5.1) can contribute significantly to a transition to a circular economy. By closing resource loops and slowing and narrowing resource flows, they can reduce the environmental impacts of production and consumption. For example, in the case of resource recovery business models, producing materials via recycling rather than from virgin materials can reduce GHG emissions significantly. Remanufacturing products that have reached their end of life can reduce the extraction of natural resources and waste generation by up to 80% relative to manufacturing new products (OECD, 2019[1]). However, the extent of the environmental benefits (as well as of the wider socio-economic impacts, including potential negative impacts) depends on the uptake of such models. In general, the market penetration of these models is currently limited. Recycling, remanufacturing and repair; the sharing of spare capacity (i.e. sharing models); and the provision of services rather than products typically only account for up to 15% of production in any given sector (OECD, 2019[1]). In recent years, some circular business models have been on the rise, largely due to the emergence of new technologies and platforms (e.g. sharing platforms such as Airbnb and car renting/sharing services). Some other business models, for example recycling and repair, are relatively mature. Circular business models have recently penetrated the market in Albania, although it remains difficult to map all the actors concerned as the vast majority of businesses are still not familiar with circular concepts and might not declare their businesses as "circular" even though they are. The main circular businesses in Albania are based on resource recovery models, mainly focusing on the reuse of agricultural surplus and by-products, sustainable packaging options, and recycled waste (particularly from vehicles or electronics) (see Annex C).

To increase the market penetration of these business models and make them more competitive with the more traditional, linear business models, countries need to implement an enabling framework in the different economic sectors that would support the adoption of such models.

Overview and approach to the selection of the proposed policy recommendations

The approach used for selecting the proposed policy recommendations for this area is a bit different from the approach used for the economic instruments and plastics priorities. The overall aim of the recommendations is to provide an enabling framework for SMEs to scale up the adoption of the five types of circular business models. The business models themselves cover the different stages of the life cycle, where, for example, the circular supplies model aims at increasing the use of secondary, bio-based or alternative materials in production, while resource recovery models focus on the end-of-life and recycling. Therefore, the recommendations aim at providing policy measures that can be applied across the five types of business models and economic sectors to support SMEs' activities (Table 5.1). Examples of international good practices in this area are focused on the key selected priorities to the extent possible, such as plastics, tourism (in particular, accommodation and food services), municipal (and industrial) waste management, and awareness raising, but they also include textiles and footwear as another key economic sector in Albania.

The proposed policy recommendations primarily target the supply side of circular business models, namely SMEs. For a small, tourism-dependent economy like Albania, boosting the economic growth of SMEs that does not come at an environmental cost is particularly pertinent. The pandemic has put additional pressure on Albanian SMEs and their greening efforts, primarily due to issues with liquidity maintenance and access to finance. Well co-ordinated and targeted financial and technical support will be required to help Albanian SMEs overcome challenges in adopting sustainable practices and circular business models. To date, incentives and instruments to encourage them to engage in greener practices remain scarce in Albania. Access to green finance is also limited, and regulatory instruments are non-existent. On a positive note, information-based tools and, in particular, awareness-raising activities, have been scaled up to some extent (OECD, 2022[3]).

Table 5.1. Overview of the proposed policy recommendations in the circular business models priority area for small and medium-sized enterprises for Albania

Short term	Medium term	Long term
Provide awareness-raising campaigns and training programmes on the circular economy for small and medium-sized enterprises (SMEs), including showcasing good practices and access to finance	Continue facilitating the exchange of practices and learning from peers, including cross-sectoral knowledge development	Consider additional investment support for SMEs (e.g. accelerated depreciation rate, guarantee schemes, tax incentives)
Introduce calls for circular business models projects within existing and new funding programmes	Provide support to SMEs on environmental legislation and obligations to ease their administrative burden	Organise investor-entrepreneur matchmaking events
Provide financial, combined with technical, assistance to SMEs (business support, access to finance support)	Support capacity building and entrepreneurship skills as well as vocational training	
Support collaboration between SMEs and academia, as well as regional and international collaboration on research and development and innovation		
Establish a circular economy stakeholder/business platform to strengthen collaboration within and across value chains		
Consider establishing a dedicated funding programme for SMEs to scale up circular business models		

However, the consumer side also needs to be addressed in parallel to increase the demand for green products and services. More extensive use of economic instruments for a circular economy (see Chapter 4) can also help scale up these business models, as economic instruments change the relative price of different products and services and can, hence, make circular business models more price-competitive compared to more linear business models.

Key proposed policy recommendations

The key proposed recommendations are structured according to the type of policy instrument:

1. financial support measures
2. multi-stakeholder co-operation within and across value chains
3. awareness-raising initiatives, education and other information tools.

1. Providing financial support for scaling up circular business models

The transition to a circular economy requires resources to drive the uptake of new business models, support the development of innovative technologies and motivate behavioural change within society. Governments can support the transition to a circular economy by using specific economic instruments (see Chapter 4). Another way for governments to help reorient market forces towards a circular economy is by providing financial support for projects and initiatives through grants and loans. These instruments help decrease the cost of capital for circular investments and overcome financial and information barriers. Public funding can thereby stimulate the development of new circular business models, innovative technologies and strategic partnerships. The diagnostics that the OECD prepared in the context of developing this roadmap (see Chapter 2) showed that SMEs in Albania report increased costs and a lack of government subsidies as being the most significant impediments to adopting circular business models (RCC, 2023[7]). The review of the availability of financial incentives for green investments for SMEs in Albania also indicated that Albania has yet not established adequate national mechanisms to provide financial incentives for SME greening (OECD, 2022[3]). Albania will thus need to provide financial support for scaling up circular business models. In the context of this roadmap, this can be done in four ways.

In the short term, Albania could introduce calls for circular business models projects within existing and new funding programmes that provide grants and soft loans. Such projects could be integrated as part of the green finance envisaged by the new Business Development and Investment Strategy (2021-2027). Moreover, as the Albanian Investment Development Agency revitalises some of its grant support schemes to increase SMEs' competitiveness and innovation capacity, a specific amount of total financing could be dedicated to circular projects. These calls should specify the priorities and the allocation of funds dedicated to circular economy projects. The focus of supported projects could be the introduction of new business models, including eco-innovation, and pilot projects and knowledge dissemination in the areas of the circular economy. The call could also specify preference for projects with a focus on plastics, textiles, municipal waste management and tourism as key priorities for Albania. For example, agritourism businesses could be supported in implementing circular measures, such as composting facilities. Agritourism is an emerging business industry and a catalyst for rural development, in particular in southern Albania, and a potential priority area under the Albanian Smart Specialisation Strategy that is currently under preparation (FAO and RASP, 2020[8]).

Box 5.1 provides an example of how circular business models were integrated within existing and new funding programmes in Hungary. Hungary used the process of developing a national circular economy strategy to identify the circular economy priorities that would be included in the existing funding programme (funded by the EU Structural and Cohesion Funds) in its next programming period, 2021-27. It then organised an awareness-raising and training event for SMEs in the country to instigate applications for this programme and the circular economy priority in particular (see the section on "

3. Raising SMEs' awareness and education on the circular economy").

Box 5.1. Introducing calls for projects focused on circular business models within existing funding programmes

Hungary's Operational Programme for 2021-2027

Environmental and Energy Efficiency Operational Programme (EEEOP) Plus in Hungary

The EEEOP Plus is the continuation of the previous EEEOP under the new framework for the period 2021-27 (as illustrated in Figure 5.2). Its priorities include:

- water management and disaster risk reduction
- circular economy systems and sustainability
- protection of the environment and nature
- a renewable energy economy
- a just transition.

The Operational Programme's overall budget is HUF 1 612.56 billion (EUR 4.3 billion), with HUF 411.97 billion (EUR 1.1 billion) allocated to the priority covering circular economy systems and sustainability, including:

- Under the waste management objective, the programme funds projects with a focus on improving the existing separate waste collection system; supporting waste recycling and the production of high-quality secondary raw materials; developing new waste management centres and upgrading existing ones; optimising municipal waste collection and transport; supporting residual waste facilities; rehabilitating abandoned old landfills; and active, experience-based, community-building awareness-raising activities.
- The circular economy-related objective is a new topic of the Operational Programme. Its aim is to pave the way for a circular transition through small-scale investments mainly targeting small and medium-sized enterprises. The funding focuses on service provision; promoting a decoupling of raw material consumption and gross domestic product growth; building value chains/circles; and developing new business sectors and business models. It targets a diverse range of projects, translating circular economy principles into practice (from both upstream and downstream perspectives); awareness-raising activities; and small demonstration/pilot projects.

Figure 5.2. EEEOP Plus and its precursor EEEOP

EEEOP 2014-2020

Priority	Action	Alloc. EUR M	Main respon-sible
1	Water management	891	MoI
	Disaster management/Climate	154	
2	Drinking water	183	MTI
	Waste water	1 031	
3	Waste management	300	MTI
	Remediation	100	MTI
4	Nature protection	100	MoA
5	Renewable energy	314	MTI
	Energy efficiency	600	
	District heating	106	
	Awareness raising	6	
	TOTAL	**3 785**	

EEEOP Plus 2021-2027

Priority	Action	Alloc. EUR M	Main respon-sible
1	Water management	702	MoI
	Disaster management/Climate	121	
2	Sustainable water utility systems	652	MTI
	Green and blue infrastructure	190	
	Circular waste management	208	
	Circular economy	52	
3	Remediation/Environmental protection	45	MoA
	Nature protection	112	
4	Promoting energy efficiency measures	883	MTI
	Promoting renewable energy	535	
	Smart energy systems, -networks and -storage	518	
5	Just Transition Fund	295	MTI
	TOTAL	**4 313**	

Note: MoI: Ministry of Interior; MTI: Ministry of Technology and Innovation; MoA: Ministry of Agriculture.
Source: Prime Minister's Office, Hungary.

Table 5.2 summarises the indicators and targets for these two objectives.

Table 5.2. Indicators and targets of waste and circular economy-related actions within the EEEOP Plus

Specific objective	Action	Indicator		Unit	Baseline		Milestone 2024	Target 2029
		Code	Name		Value	Year		
2.3. Transition to a circular economy	Circular waste management	RCO34	Additional capacity for waste recycling	tonnes/year	n.r.	n.r.	50 000	250 000
		RCR47	Waste recycled	tonnes/year	0	2021	n.r.	300 000
	Circular economy	RC001	Enterprises supported	number	n.r.	n.r.	16	160
		RCR04	Small and medium-sized enterprises introducing marketing or organisational innovation	number	0	2021	n.r.	143

Note: n.r.: not reported.
Source: Prime Minister's Office, Hungary; OECD (2023[9]).

The financial support in the form of grants and loans should be combined with technical and other assistance to SMEs. This non-financial support could consist of more general business support (e.g. to write a good business plan or access-to-finance support) as well as of technical support through consultancy services in the area of circular business models. Such support could be offered through business incubators or accelerators (such as UpLiftAlbania acceleration programme or Growpreneur). It is common practice in some programmes funded by international development co-operation partners that more general business as well as technical support be provided in addition to a grant and/or a soft loan. For example, the European Bank for Reconstruction and Development administers energy efficiency programmes that provide a small non-reimbursable grant, a soft loan and consulting services to successful applicants and training to financial institutions that administer those loans locally. Scotland has set up the Circular Economy Business Support Service to provide one-on-one consultancy for SMEs across all sectors (Zero Waste Scotland, 2020[10]) while Luxembourg has set up a decision-making tool (Fit4Circularity) through which it helps companies identify and assess their growth potential, and adopt circular economy approaches and innovative business models (Luxinnovation, 2020[11]).

In the short term, Albania could consider establishing a dedicated funding programme for SMEs to scale up circular business models. Some progress has been made in this respect at the subnational level. For example, the municipality of Tirana provided financial support for 2021-23 to new green businesses based on eco-friendly business models or existing businesses that aspire to develop green products or services (OECD, 2022[3]). The total amount of the fund is EUR 347 500, and each beneficiary will be supported with direct grants of EUR 4 800, with an aid intensity of 80% of eligible costs. Such an initiative could be also considered at the national level and could be implemented by the Albanian Investment Development Agency (AIDA). For example, within the RE:Source innovation programme, the Swedish government has appointed two agencies to invest in a strategic innovation programme that focuses on developing a circular economy and resource efficiency innovations (RE:Source, n.d.[12]). This programme brings together companies, universities and authorities to collaborate in strategically important areas and provides specific funding for projects under this programme and five platforms to develop solutions for its priority areas. Another example is from Scotland, which has set up a Circular Economy Investment Fund offering a grant to SMEs and non-governmental organisations for innovative circular economy projects resulting from the Circular Economy Business Support Service and nearing commercialisation (Zero Waste Scotland, n.d.[13]). In Albania, the focus could be, for example, on launching circular construction and renovation pilots in the tourism sector or circular business models aimed at food waste prevention. An example of such a model is a food waste prevention app, similar to the Danish Too Good To Go, which allows users to browse unsold food items in nearby shops and restaurants at discounted prices (Too Good To Go, n.d.[14]). To implement such a programme in Albania will probably require that the programme be funded and administered by international development co-operation partners. Also, Albanian SMEs will need to have achieved a certain level of knowledge and experience to ensure that the programme generates a pipeline of circular economy projects with good business plans that are economically and financially sustainable (see the section on 3. Raising SMEs' awareness and education on the circular economy).

In the long term, Albania could consider additional investment support for SMEs (e.g. accelerated depreciation and guarantee schemes as well as other tax incentives). The review of the Albanian state-of-play on financial incentives available for SME greening found that only a few guarantee funds operating in Albania cover green investments, such as the Albanian Agribusiness Support Facility and the KfW-supported Rural Credit Guarantee Fund with its dedicated "green window", and they only have limited uptake (OECD, 2022[3]). Once some progress has been made on scaling up circular business models in Albania, it could consider modifying the corporate income tax system to provide tax benefits for SMEs engaging in research and development activities related to circular economy solutions or for investments in environmentally friendly technologies. For example, the Netherlands has two such schemes: 1) the Environmental Investment Deduction Scheme (MIA scheme) allows an entrepreneur to deduct up to 36% of the investment costs for an environmentally friendly investment on top of the regular investment tax deduction; 2) the Arbitrary Depreciation of Environmental Investments Scheme (Vamil scheme) allows the entrepreneur to decide when to write off 75% of the investment costs, thereby providing an advantage with regard to liquidity and interest (Netherlands Enterprise Agency, n.d.[15]).

2. Establishing and strengthening multi-stakeholder co-operation within and across value chains

Strengthening collaboration among the relevant stakeholders and partnerships between public and private organisations is key for transitioning to a circular economy. Transitioning to a circular economy will require a change across the entire economy. Promoting inter-sectoral, cross-agency and interdepartmental collaboration in Albania would help scale up innovative circular business models, as the circular economy concept cuts across economic sectors and value chains as well as the competencies of public authorities. Currently, the poor co-ordination among institutional, civil society, academia and private sector stakeholders hampers the proper implementation of green policies (OECD, 2022[3]). Efforts in this regard should be spearheaded by the recently formed Directorate for Circular Economy, operating under the Ministry of Tourism and Environment. Additionally, the working group established during the development of this roadmap could play a central role in these initiatives. To improve multi-stakeholder co-operation within and across value chains, Albania could focus on three key actions.

In the short term, Albania will need to establish a circular economy stakeholder/business platform to strengthen collaboration, information exchange and the exchange of good practices. Besides enabling collaboration and networking opportunities between the public and private sectors, such platforms (whether virtual or physical) may also facilitate synergies and knowledge-sharing across the different parts of the value chain. A circular economy stakeholder platform, established as part of the OECD project "Supporting Green Transition through Circular Economy Roadmaps", can provide a solid foundation for such efforts (see Annex A for more information). Some have set up working groups to work on specific topics. Most European countries have established national circular economy stakeholder platforms or hubs, which serve as fora for information exchange; peer learning; multi-stakeholder co-operation; and a depository of information, data and other relevant material (see Box 5.2 for a few examples). Albania could set up a specific working group for the tourism sector, where SMEs could discuss and exchange practices on sustainable tourism practices, for example in the accommodation and food services sub-sectors. In particular, regarding the food system, evidence shows that a joint vision and joint action are needed to create commitment and to achieve the overarching goals and targets, as the underlying causes and challenges of food waste are complex and linked to other issues related to food health and safety and food resilience and security. In such an intertwined value chain, each stakeholder has a role to play but cannot act without collaborating with the other relevant actors (OECD, 2022[16]).

Box 5.2. Examples of circular economy platforms/hubs

- **Slovak Circular Economy Platform** (Circular Slovakia) – established in the form of a public-private partnership by the Slovak Ministry of Environment, the Embassy of the Kingdom of the Netherlands, the Institute for Circular Economy, PwC Slovakia, the Slovak Business Agency and the Slovak Environment Agency in 2019. Its main goals are to promote a circular economy to businesses as an approach that provides economic benefits and opportunities, exchange, information and experience; help build business partnerships and new projects; inform businesses about the latest legislation in the area; and support their participation in the policy-making process. The platform also helps increase discussion between the public and private sectors as well as among businesses themselves.
- **Circular Glasgow** – hosted since 2015 by the Glasgow Chamber of Commerce, Zero Waste Scotland and the Glasgow City Council (United Kingdom). Circular Glasgow aims to build best practices and capacity on the circular economy across Glasgow businesses, helping them identify opportunities to support and implement circular ideas. This is done through workshops and events – a series of knowledge-sharing business-to-business networking events; a circle assessment – a tool which helps businesses understand opportunities to become more circular; and the Circle Lab – an online hackathon event to find circular solutions to local challenges.
- The **Italian Circular Economy Stakeholder Platform** – established in 2018 by the National Agency for New Technologies, Energy and Sustainable Economic Development, as a mirror initiative of the European Circular Economy Stakeholder Platform. It acts through six working groups: 1) Research and eco-innovation, dissemination of knowledge and training; 2) Regulatory and Economic tools; 3) Tools for measuring the circular economy; 4) Sustainable and circular value chains; 5) Circular Cities and Territories; and 6) Good practices and Integrated Approaches. The platform aims to foster synergies between relevant stakeholders, overcome the fragmentation of initiatives at the Italian level, map good practices, and promote the Italian way for the circular economy at the national and international level.
- **Türkiye Circular Economy Platform** – established in 2020 by the Business Council for Sustainable Development of Türkiye. The platform aims to provide practical solutions, incentives, news and opportunities in the field of the circular economy. It includes a knowledge hub, an e-commerce platform for industrial symbiosis (as part of Türkiye Materials Marketplace – established in 2016) and measurement tools and offers training, financial opportunities and consultancy services for companies looking to accelerate their circular transition.
- Other examples of platforms connecting experts and organisations, engaging stakeholders within different working groups, and promoting projects that integrate the principles of a circular economy include the Holland Circular Hotspot and the newly established Czech Circular Hotspot.

Sources: OECD (2021[17]); ICESP (n.d.[18]) ; BCSD (n.d.[19]); INCIEN (2021[20]); Holland Circular Hotspot (2022[21])

Albania should also strengthen collaboration between SMEs and academia, as well as regional and international collaboration on R&D and innovation. Collaboration between SMEs and academia could be improved, for example, by introducing grants for collaborative R&D, innovation vouchers or supporting the establishment of collaborative research centres. For instance, in the United Kingdom, funding is available through the TSB Collaborative R&D Scheme to encourage collaboration between business and researchers. The Czech Republic implements a government programme for applied research and experimental development administered by the Technology Agency of the Czech Republic. In particular, its ZETA programme supports co-operation between academia and industry (Technology Agency of the Czech Republic, n.d.[22]). A guide on setting up collaborations for a circular economy can be found in the

Circle Economy's recent publication (2020[23]). This objective can also be achieved by incorporating a circular component into the portfolios of existing initiatives, such as Tirana-Inc. The programme, established in 2021 through collaboration among Albania's five leading universities with support from the EU for Innovation project, aims to foster entrepreneurship and innovation among university students by providing training, working spaces and advice. Moreover, Albania could promote more regional and international collaboration, for example, by sharing examples of regional and international projects and helping SMEs to establish partnerships with other businesses or academia. This could be done through their national contact points for EU programmes (e.g. Horizon Europe).

In the long term, and once circular business models are more known and widespread in Albania, the country could also organise investor-entrepreneur matchmaking events. The aim of these events would be to gather investors and innovators in Albania, present the pipeline of potential projects that support circular business models, pitch the ideas to investors and try to match investors with project developers. This is more common for technological innovations in the energy sector, but the same concept has been expanded to circular innovations as well (for example, in Germany and the Netherlands). Public authorities can be involved in setting up such business support networks, as is the case in the Netherlands (e.g. the Ministry of Infrastructure and Water has jointly created with other partners the Netherlands Circular Accelerator business platform that helps match entrepreneurs across regions and value chains). Such events could also be organised regionally (in the Western Balkans), where the aim would be to establish new connections and joint investments across the region.

3. Raising SMEs' awareness and education on the circular economy

Chapter 2's diagnostics show that only 44% of SMEs have a clear understanding of the circular economy and only 20% of businesses believe that their business models contribute to a circular economy. Moderate efforts have been made to raise awareness of the benefits of greening activities among SMEs, such as cost savings and increased productivity (OECD, 2022[3]). Awareness-raising activities have been conducted through different campaigns with the support of international partners. Some capacity-building workshops with local governments and the private sector have also been undertaken. Moreover, the annual Green Businesses award competition is organised to raise awareness and encourage SME eco-innovation, aiming to serve as an incubator for small-scale green development ideas, using local resources and reviving the traditions of production and community-based markets in an environmentally friendly way. Awareness-raising activities are also part of the new Business Development and Investment Strategy (2021-2027) (OECD, 2022[3]). To further support the scaling up of circular business models, Albania will need to continuously implement targeted communication and education initiatives. This could also be done through private sector organisations, including chambers of commerce.

In the short term, Albania should focus on raising awareness on the circular economy and circular business models for SMEs through additional communication campaigns and training programmes, including by showcasing good practices and access-to-finance possibilities. Such activities could be conducted by AIDA, considering its expanding role as a government business support services provider, as envisaged in the Business Development and Investment Strategy (2021-2027). AIDA's Access to Finance portal, established in 2021 as a one-stop shop on financial support for SMEs, can also serve as a good avenue to showcase financing options that target the circular economy. Apart from AIDA, both the Union of Chambers of Commerce and Industry of Albania and the Chamber of Commerce and Industry of Tirana, which already provide support services to SMEs, could offer further training on circular business models. Awareness-raising and educational activities could focus on circular business models in general or aim at specific sectors. In collaboration with the Hungarian Prime Minister's Office, the OECD organised a training event in Hungary as part of a project supporting the development of the national circular economy strategy. The event aimed to raise awareness and provide training on circular business models, particularly for small and medium-sized enterprises. It introduced the Circular Economy Technology Platform, outlined circular economy principles for key priority areas (construction, biomass and food, and plastics), and highlighted successful examples of circular business models in Hungary. The session concluded with a presentation on public funding opportunities for transitioning to a circular economy in Hungary. Albania could consider organising a similar event focusing on specific economic sectors and value chains, such as plastics, tourism and textiles.

In the medium term, Albania will need to continue facilitating the exchange of practices and peer learning, including cross-sectoral knowledge development. This could be done through dedicated stakeholder events and campaigns on specific topics (for example, on food waste prevention in the tourism sector) or through a circular economy platform/hub (see also Box 5.2). There are ample examples of international good practices on food waste prevention information campaigns. The campaigns, including the involvement of retail and food services, would help target consumer campaigns and interactive events around action-oriented policy measures. The Albanian authorities could also collaborate with the food industry and the non-governmental sector on promoting food waste reduction strategies directed at consumers, develop a best practices inventory or (online) resource database accessible to consumers and professionals, and support the training and education of food professionals and employees. Regarding the textiles sector, for instance, the WRAP "Love Your Clothes" campaign in the United Kingdom is an example of an awareness-raising campaign about the value of clothes and how their lifetime can be extended, aiming to encourage people to make the most of them. Other examples include advising services and workshops offered within the "Repaired Better Than New" initiative in the Metropolitan Area of Barcelona (Spain) and the Repair Café International Foundation in the Netherlands.

In the medium term, Albania could also provide support to SMEs on environmental legislation and obligations to ease their administrative burden. This would entail providing an overview and advice on environmental obligations and policy developments. This is particularly relevant to SMEs, as they often lack adequate resources and capacities and are less likely to follow policy developments and legislative initiatives. This can be achieved by, for example, integrating this information and advice within a circular economy platform, funding programme or as part of awareness-raising campaigns. Circular economy and waste-related stakeholder events often include sessions that provide an overview of legislative changes, new reporting obligations and the impact this may have on businesses. Circular economy platforms or hubs also tend to have a dedicated section on their website that summarises key legislation and obligations. It can also be part of an extended producer responsibility scheme, where producer responsibility organisations disseminate such information to their members.

Albania could also support capacity building and entrepreneurship skills as well as vocational training on the circular economy. Education and capacity-building instruments include tailored training courses for companies and entrepreneurs and advice/consulting support for start-ups, companies and entrepreneurs that can be provided by a variety of institutions in the country or within international projects funded by international development co-operation partners. Local authorities and/or waste management organisations can also facilitate the education activities by sending representatives to schools or inviting children to facility tours. Producers under the extended producer responsibility are also obliged to finance such educational activities. In some countries, compulsory minimum producer responsibility obligation expenditures spent on awareness have also been introduced. In Austria, they amount to 0.3% of income; in Poland it is 5% (Drab, Engel and Kristofory, 2020[24]).

International projects relevant to the circular economy and waste could have a component dedicated to the provision of training to local SMEs as well as financial institutions to raise awareness and knowledge among entrepreneurs about circular business models on the one hand and educate investors about the risks and opportunities of such projects on the other, hence, increasing the likelihood of financing such projects. The Circular Economy Regional Initiative funded by the European Bank for Reconstruction and Development and the Global Environmental Facility seeks to drive the expansion of the circular economy in the Western Balkans and Türkiye by focusing efforts on decreasing the barriers to investments in circular business models, technologies and processes. As one of its main components, the project contributes to active knowledge sharing between relevant stakeholders and offers technical assistance necessary for developing bankable projects (GEF, 2021[25]). This is one example of common practice in programmes funded by international development co-operation partners, though most are aimed at increasing energy efficiency and renewable energies. Awareness-raising initiatives and education activities are especially relevant for SMEs and start-ups, which, besides their already lower exposure to domestic R&D and innovation activities, might also not be fully aware of the opportunities offered by circular business models and might lack skills in accessing and using existing data, information and knowledge.

References

BCSD (n.d.), "Turkey Circular Economy Platform", https://donguselekonomiplatformu.com/en (accessed on 1 December 2023). [19]

Circle Economy (2020), *Will You Be My Partner? Nine Steps to Identify and Establish Successful Collaborations for a Circular Economy*, Circle Economy, https://www.circle-economy.com/resources/will-you-be-my-partner-collaborations-in-the-circular-economy. [23]

Drab, J., M. Engel and T. Kristofory (2020), *Sorting Out Waste Sorting*, Institute for Environmental Policy, Ministry of the Environment of the Slovak Republic, https://www.minzp.sk/files/iep/sorting_out_waste_sorting.pdf. [24]

FAO and RASP (2020), *Agritourism Development in Albania: Case of Malësi e Madhe, Belsh and Korça Regions*, Food and Agriculture Organization, https://rasp.org.al/wp-content/uploads/2023/01/Position-paper-on-Agriturism-in-Albania.pdf. [8]

GEF (2021), *Circular Economy Regional Initiative (CERI)*, https://www.thegef.org/projects-operations/projects/10328. [25]

Government of Albania (2021), *Business Development and Investment Strategy 2021-2027*, Government of Albania, Tirana, http://qbz.gov.al/eli/vendim/2021/07/30/466. [4]

Holland Circular Hotspot (2022), *Construction*, https://hollandcircularhotspot.nl/themes/construction (accessed on 31 January 2022). [21]

ICESP (n.d.), "Italian platform of actors for the circular economy", web page, https://www.icesp.it (accessed on 25 November 2023). [18]

ICT (2021), *SME Competitiveness Outlook 2021: Empowering the Green Recovery*, International Trade Centre, Geneva, https://www.intracen.org/publications/smeco2021/ITCSMECO2021. [5]

INCIEN (2021), "INCIEN is starting the Czech circular hotspot in the new year – will you be a part of it?", web page, https://www.enviweb.cz/rss/256996. [20]

Lacy, P. and J. Rutqvist (2015), *Waste to Wealth: The Circular Economy Advantage*, Springer. [2]

Luxinnovation (2020), "Performance programmes Fit 4 Circularity", https://www.luxinnovation.lu/innovate-in-luxembourg/fit-4-performance-programmes. [11]

Netherlands Enterprise Agency (n.d.), "MIA and Vamil", https://english.rvo.nl/subsidies-programmes/mia-and-vamil (accessed on 3 June 2021). [15]

OECD (2023), *Towards a National Circular Economy Strategy for Hungary*, OECD Publishing, Paris, https://doi.org/10.1787/1178c379-en. [9]

OECD (2022), "Closing the loop in the Slovak Republic: A roadmap towards circularity for competitiveness, eco-innovation and sustainability", *OECD Environment Policy Papers*, No. 30, OECD Publishing, Paris, https://doi.org/10.1787/acadd43a-en. [16]

OECD (2022), *SME Policy Index: Western Balkans and Turkey 2022: Assessing the Implementation of the Small Business Act for Europe*, SME Policy Index, OECD Publishing, Paris, https://doi.org/10.1787/b47d15f0-en. [3]

OECD (2021), "No net zero without SMEs: Exploring the key issues for greening SMEs and green entrepreneurship", *OECD SME and Entrepreneurship Papers*, No. 30, OECD Publishing, Paris, https://doi.org/10.1787/bab63915-en. [6]

OECD (2021), *The Circular Economy in Glasgow, United Kingdom*, OECD Urban Studies, OECD Publishing, Paris, https://doi.org/10.1787/7717a310-en. [17]

OECD (2019), *Business Models for the Circular Economy: Opportunities and Challenges for Policy*, OECD Publishing, Paris, https://doi.org/10.1787/g2g9dd62-en. [1]

RCC (2023), *Balkan Business Barometer Opinion 2023*, Regional Cooperation Council, Sarajevo, https://www.rcc.int/balkanbarometer/results/1/business. [7]

RE:Source (n.d.), *RE:Source website*, https://resource-sip.se. [12]

Technology Agency of the Czech Republic (n.d.), "Programmes and challenges", web page, https://www.tacr.cz/programy-a-souteze/programy (accessed on 2 March 2022). [22]

Too Good To Go (n.d.), "Luttons contre le gaspillage alimentaire ensemble", https://www.toogoodtogo.com/fr (accessed on 15 January 2024). [14]

Zero Waste Scotland (2020), "Circular Economy Business Support Service", web page, https://www.zerowastescotland.org.uk/circular-economy/business-support-service (accessed on 3 June 2021). [10]

Zero Waste Scotland (n.d.), "Circular Economy Investment Fund", web page, https://www.zerowastescotland.org.uk (accessed on 3 June 2021). [13]

6 Plastics, with a focus on marine litter

This chapter focuses on the priority area that seeks to achieve a more circular plastics life cycle in Albania, with particular attention on marine litter and most common applications of plastics in packaging, construction and single-use plastic products. It provides a synopsis of the current developments and challenges within the existing policy landscape, highlights areas requiring improvement, and puts forth a set of policy recommendations supported by international good practices.

Circular economy in the plastics life cycle

Plastics are highly versatile, light and affordable. They are found in numerous applications, such as in packaging, construction, transportation, fishing and electronics. However, the widespread use of plastics has raised significant environmental concerns throughout the entire life cycle of the material (Figure 6.1) (OECD, 2022[1]). The circular economy can help minimise these environmental impacts by closing the plastics loop.

There are many opportunities to make plastics' life cycle more circular (OECD, 2023[2]), including:

- **More circular design:** A plastic product is designed to be used and reused over a long period of time. Once it becomes waste, it can be easily sorted, separately processed without cross-contamination and recycled.
- **Use of secondary feedstock in production:** A plastic product is manufactured from secondary plastics, whenever possible (if the technical features and requirements of the product allow). If primary feedstock is used for manufacturing, the harmful chemicals and additives that hamper recyclability should be avoided.
- **Longer use and more reuse:** A more circular use of plastics ensures that plastic products stay in use for as long as possible. Products with long lifetimes and high reusability are favoured over single-use plastics with short lifetimes. Products that can be disassembled, and whose parts are reused, repaired and replaced if they become obsolete or non-functional, are also treated preferentially.
- **End-of-life management:** A circular end-of-life treatment of plastics means ensuring that a large percentage of plastics is recycled once a product is discarded. This means a higher rate of separate collection, a higher purity of sorted plastic waste and thus, a higher quality of secondary plastic. Plastic waste that cannot be recycled is treated and leakage to the environment avoided.

Figure 6.1. The circular plastics life cycle keeps materials in a closed loop

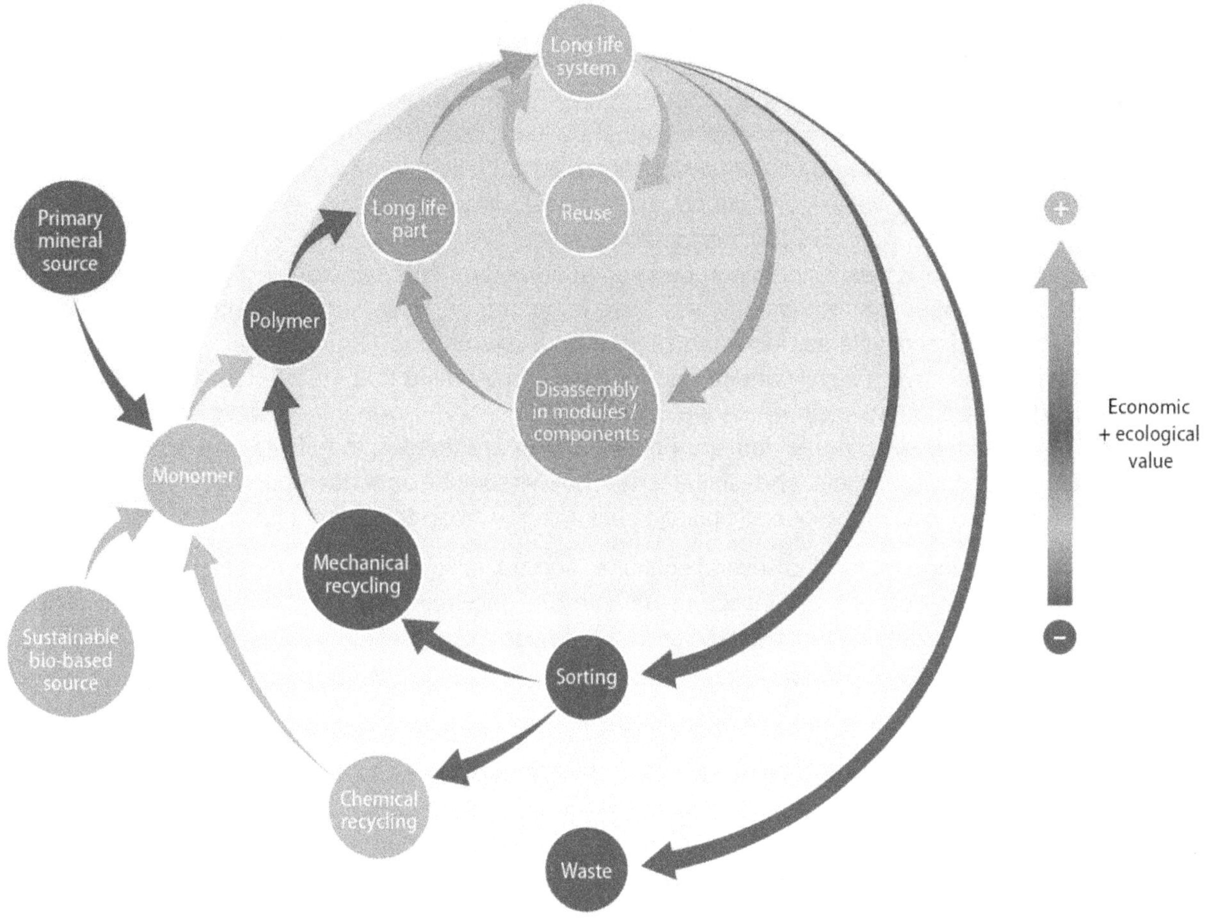

Source: Adapted from OECD (2023[2]).

Motivations for the selection of plastics, with a focus on marine litter as a key priority area of the Roadmap

Plastics in Albania are assessed as a priority area with high policy relevance. Albania will need to implement national obligations and targets related to plastics. Namely, its National Plan for Integrated Waste Management (2020-2035) foresees specific targets for the recovery of plastic packaging waste generated (10% by 2025, 12% by 2030 and 22.5% by 2035). Albania will also need to align its regulatory framework with the European Union's (EU) plastics legislation, in line with its EU accession negotiations. EU plastics legislation contains a number of obligations and targets, including minimum recycling targets for plastic packaging materials, a separate collection target and minimum recycled plastic content for plastic bottles, as well as a ban on certain single-use plastic products. While Albania's waste law has been amended to ban the production, import and sale of certain categories of single-use plastic bags, more alignment with EU legislation will be needed. A task force has been established to ensure the enforcement of the ban and impose penalties for non-compliance.[1] In addition, on a regional level, this topic is an important element of the circular economy pillar of the Green Agenda of the Western Balkans and the related Action Plan until 2030. In this context, Albania, together with the five other Western Balkans economies, issued a joint statement on prevention of plastic pollution, including marine litter, at the Berlin Process Summit 2023 (Berlin Process Summit, 2023[3]). On a global level, there is also an ongoing negotiation for an internationally legally binding instrument to address plastic pollution that has attracted the attention of global leaders.

Waste data in Albania are still not considered of high quality (see Chapter 4), in particular when it comes to specific waste streams. According to the available estimates, plastic waste constitutes a relatively small share of generated waste (around 9.2%). Moreover, while comprehensive estimates of the amount of recycled plastics are lacking, overall recycling rates are very low in Albania (17%) and the majority of plastics is collected for recycling by the informal sector. Albania is also one of the economies with large proportions of mismanaged waste, contributing to a high leakage of (often untreated) plastic waste into the Adriatic-Ionian basin, amounting to 20 kg per person per year (World Bank, 2020[4]), with litter from fishing and shipping in the Adriatic Sea further compounding the problem. This may result in plastic pollution and leakage from mismanaged plastic waste, which have important negative environmental implications and may harm nature and ecosystems, including marine ecosystems and human health. Throughout their life cycle, plastics also have a significant carbon footprint, contributing to 3.4% of global greenhouse gas emissions in 2019 throughout their whole life cycle (OECD, 2022[1]). Albania has only recently started working on policy instruments in this domain. Further efforts are needed to fulfil its ambition to meet the relevant national and EU targets and obligations. The circularity and decarbonisation potential and strategic importance of plastics, especially plastic packaging, is, therefore, very high in Albania.

Plastics are also a strategic material to several economic sectors, in spite of their lower economic importance. The most important applications of plastics in Albania are packaging, textile, construction and fishing. Plastics' usage, in particular single-use plastic products, is also exacerbated by the growing tourism sector.

Overview and approach to the selection of the proposed policy recommendations

The approach to the selection of the proposed policy recommendations for the plastics priority area is similar to that for the priority area on economic instruments. Recommendations advocate a life cycle approach with a focus on design, production, (re)use and end-of-life stages. This is because the entire plastics life cycle, from the extraction of feedstock materials to the end-of-life stage, create significant environmental pressures affecting ecosystem health, economic growth and human well-being, as highlighted above. The proposed measures also aim to bridge the gap between the current situation in Albania and plastics obligations and targets stemming from national and EU legislation. They also aim to tap the high circularity potential this area offers (see Table 6.1), including reduced use of single-use plastics, increased recycling of plastics packaging and reduced plastic leakage into the environment, including the aquatic environment.

This priority area also integrates measures related to the use of plastics that can contribute to improved municipal waste management, a more sustainable tourism sector and increased awareness of the circular economy transition in Albania (Table 6.1).

Table 6.1. Overview of the proposed policy recommendations in the plastics priority area

Short term	Medium term	Long term
Improve municipal waste management in general	Introduce eco-modulated fees for plastic packaging within the EPR scheme for packaging	Support and scale up innovation into more recyclable plastic materials, plastics recycling technologies and processes as well as plastics reuse and reduction
Improve separate collection of plastic waste and other packaging	Develop a strategy to curb plastic pollution, including marine plastic litter	Introduce minimum recycled content requirements for specific plastic waste streams
Raise awareness and educate businesses, public authorities and households on plastic waste prevention, circular design and littering	Use green public procurement to favour reusable and recycled plastics	Consider taxes on virgin and non-recycled plastics
Implement an extended producer responsibility (EPR) take-back scheme for packaging (including plastic packaging)	Consider a deposit-refund system for plastic bottles	
Introduce taxes and/or bans on certain single-use plastics		

Key proposed policy recommendations

The proposed policy recommendations are structured around the plastics life cycle but also include some cross-cutting measures that can be applied across the plastics life cycle:

1. measures to close the plastics loop at the end-of-life phase and increase plastics recycling
2. measures focused on longer use and more reuse of plastics to shift demand from single-use plastics to alternatives and facilitate reuse and repair
3. measures targeting design and production to curb virgin plastics use and facilitate recycling
4. cross-cutting measures to support a transition to a more circular plastics use.

1. Closing the plastics loop through increased recycling and better waste management

As explained in Chapter 2, Albania faces several challenges with waste management, including municipal waste management. Better waste management and increased recycling in general are crucial to closing the plastics loop and to ensuring that there is a sufficient amount of recycled plastics material available for substituting virgin plastics more upstream in the value chain. This can be achieved through multiple and complementing policy measures aimed at the end-of-life phase of plastics products.

In the short term, Albania will need to improve municipal waste management in general. A mix of policy instruments is needed to achieve better (plastic) waste management. Legislation needs to provide clear definitions and obligations for private actors and municipalities as well as a monitoring and enforcement systems to monitor compliance. Awareness-raising instruments are needed to educate plastic waste generators, including households, on how to separate and dispose of waste (see Section "4. Cross-cutting measures"). Economic instruments are complementary tools that provide economic incentives for private actors to improve their environmental performance and help them achieve their obligations in a cost-effective manner (see Chapter 4).

Albania should focus on two key areas of improvement in the short term. **First, separate collection of plastic (and other packaging) waste must be improved, as it is a crucial pre-condition for plastic waste recycling and the generation of high-quality secondary material.** This will also require that adequate plastic waste collection and treatment infrastructure be in place across the country to cope with the increased amount of separately collected plastic waste in an environmentally sound manner. Municipal waste separation at source and relevant infrastructure is currently almost non-existent in Albania, despite a legal obligation to do so. The main method of managing municipal waste remains disposal to landfills –

with around 60% of waste disposed of at illegal landfills (EEA, 2021[5]). The collection of plastic waste for recycling is mainly carried out by the informal sector. A few pilot projects are, nevertheless, underway to introduce separate collection in some Albanian cities, including for plastics. To improve the infrastructure for the separate collection of plastic waste, Albania will need to ensure a regular collection of this waste, the provision of properly sized containers, and an appropriate distance to the waste infrastructure or a "door-to-door" collection. It will also require education of and incentives for households to separate their plastic waste (e.g. through household waste charges). Citizen co-operation is crucial for the successful separate collection of plastic waste (and other packaging waste) in municipalities. Separate waste collection at source contributes to better waste management, but it does not necessarily reduce the amount of waste produced. It does, however, allow municipalities to reach goals that are higher up in the waste hierarchy, shifting away from landfill and incineration. Efforts to promote separate waste collection should, therefore, be integrated with actions that reduce the generation of waste itself.

Second, Albania must implement an EPR take-back scheme for packaging, including plastic packaging, to shift the waste management costs to producers and importers of plastic products (under the polluter-pays principle)[2]. An EPR scheme for packaging waste is planned to be introduced in Albania in the upcoming period, following the development of the Law on EPR, planned to be adopted at the beginning of 2024. Chapter 4 provides a more detailed discussion of EPR take-back schemes. It also provides some key elements that need to be in place to facilitate an effective implementation of EPR take-back schemes. There is also a wealth of experience with implementing EPR take-back schemes for packaging. The Czech EPR for packaging can be regarded as a good practice example (Box 6.1).

Box 6.1. Czech extended producer responsibility system for packaging

Recycling data show that the extended producer responsibility (EPR) system for packaging and packaging waste works well in the Czech Republic, and consumers effectively sort their packaging waste. For the moment, there is only one producer responsibility organisation operating on the market, EKO-KOM, covering 93% of all packaging waste in the country and 84% of packaging introduced onto the market in the Czech Republic is by clients participating in the EKO-KOM system. Compared to other countries, EKO-KOM has been attaining a high degree of recycling of packaging waste and is cost-effective regarding separation and recycling per inhabitant per year. The producer responsibility organisation operates efficiently and transparently, has established clear mechanisms for recovery, and meets the relatively demanding targets set for recovery and processing. Compliance by obligated firms is good and is backed up by the threat that, if manufacturers and importers do not comply with the law, retailers and distributors will be held responsible for take-back obligations. EKO-KOM works with municipalities, covering 99% of the Czech population. EKO-KOM financially contributes to municipalities to provide for separate collection and take-back of packaging. It also operates a dense network of coloured containers, supplemented by waste bag kerbside collection and other separation methods (e.g. collection yards, buy-back facilities). EKO-KOM also charges eco-modulated fees for reusable or single-use packaging and differentiates per tonne of material.

Sources: EKO-KOM (n.d.[6]); OECD (2018[7]); Monier, Hestin and Cavé (2014[8]).

In the medium term, Albania could consider introducing a deposit-refund system (DRS) for plastic bottles to increase the quantity and quality of their separate collection. DRS combine a charge on the sale of a product (deposit) which is reimbursed upon the return of the product or its packaging through an approved collection facility. This provides an incentive for consumers to bring back empty packaging, which can then be reused or recycled. High rates of return for reuse or recycling can be achieved because the refund provides consumers with an economic incentive to return items through the appropriate channels. The main drawback of the system is its high implementation cost, which makes it economically unviable to implement for a large range of products. DRS for plastic bottles have been implemented across OECD countries and would be a good starting point for Albania, as single-use plastics products for food consumption, including bottles, are among the top items ending up in the Adriatic and Ionian Sea (World Bank, 2020[4]). Box 6.2 describes a recent good practice example from the Slovak Republic.

Box 6.2. Deposit-refund system for single-use PET bottles and cans in the Slovak Republic

Act No. 302/2019 Coll. on the Deposit Refund System (DRS) for single-use packaging for beverages sets a number of separate collection targets:

- Plastic bottles: a minimum 60% of single-use plastic packaging placed on the market in a given year by weight should be separately collected by the end of 2022; 77% by the end of 2024 (this target is in line with the target set by the EU Single Use Plastics Directive); and 90% from 2027 onwards (the Directive sets this target from 2029 only).
- Metal cans: there is no target set for 2024; a minimum 70% of cans must be separately collected by the end of 2025; and 90% by the end of 2029. There is no such target at the EU level.

Decree No. 347/2019 Coll. of the Ministry of Environment of the Slovak Republic implementing certain provisions of the Act on DRS for single-use packaging for beverages sets the level of deposit and the scope of single-use packaging to which the DRS applies. The deposit must be a minimum of EUR 0.12 per plastic bottle and a minimum of EUR 0.10 per can. Based on evidence from other countries which have already implemented DRS schemes, these levels of deposit are expected to lead to a collection rate higher than 90%, which is an increase from the current 62% collection rate for PET bottles.

The new Slovak DRS for PET bottles and cans is set up in the form of a central system, often implemented in Scandinavian countries. Such a central system is composed of unions and associations of manufacturers. The role of the administrator is to co-ordinate and approve of the activities and to finance the system. The system is financed by manufacturers through an administrative fee for each plastic bottle and can. Additional costs incurred by retailers are financed by a handling fee. The selected DRS clearing organisation has set the level of deposit at EUR 0.15 per plastic bottle and per can.

Sources: Dráb and Slučiaková (2018[9]); Drab, Engel and Kristofory (2020[10]).

2. Shifting demand from single-use plastics to alternatives and more reuse

During the use phase, governments may influence consumers and the type of plastic products they purchase through several policy instruments. For Albania, two key policy recommendations are proposed, one for the short term and the other for the medium term to shift purchasing away from single-use plastic products to alternatives, such as reusable plastic products and products with recycled plastic content.

In the short term, Albania should introduce taxes and/or bans on certain single-use plastic products. Notably, Albania has already introduced a ban on light single-use plastic bags. Building on this, it may consider extending such a ban to additional single-use plastic products, in line with EU legislation. The recent boom in the tourism sector also underscores the importance of measures to mitigate the leakage of single-use plastic items associated with recreational activities, including, for example, plastic cups, containers, straws and beverage bottles. Such measures have been introduced across the European Union, also as a response to the EU Single-Use Plastics Directive. A tax is levied on the sale of products or groups of products increasing their price, and if passed on to consumers, can discourage them from buying those products. While product taxes have been primarily applied to certain plastic bags (e.g. Ireland), bans apply to a wider range of single-use plastic items. Both product taxes and bans have proved to be effective in reducing the use of single-use plastic bags. While taxes on plastic bags allow for some flexibility in the degree to which consumers (and indirectly producers) change their behaviour, a ban can achieve a reduction in the use of single-use plastic bags more rapidly. However, a ban may lead to a less cost-effective solution, as firms may incur higher compliance costs than if a tax was introduced. Well-designed taxes should lead to the use of more durable and more sustainable alternatives and level the playing field between primary and secondary plastics (OECD, 2023[2]).

In the medium term, Albania needs to use green public procurement to favour reusable plastic products and products with recycled plastic content. As outlined in Chapter 4, the purchasing power of public authorities can be used to steer greater supply and use of sustainable products and services. The demand for sustainable plastic products can be improved by introducing, for example, mandatory criteria (e.g. recycled content) on the purchase of plastic products (see also Box 6.1). These criteria can include the use of secondary materials, recycled content, or reusability and recyclability of the plastic product, among others. There are a few international best practice examples on green public procurement criteria for plastics that could guide Albania. The municipality of Lolland in Denmark, for example, has introduced recycling and recyclability criteria for packaging in its tender for cleaning services. In Sweden, green public procurement criteria related to plastics are applied in the procurement of office IT equipment. In Belgium and Germany, bans on certain single-use products have been introduced. For example, the city of Hamburg banned the use of plastic coffee capsules, single-use bottles, utensils and plates in government buildings (Watkins et al., 2019[11]). Japan also uses green public procurement criteria on plastic products, where the higher the recycled content share in an evaluated good, the higher the evaluation score for that good. For instance, stationery products should contain at least 40% recycled plastics in terms of weight.

3. Curbing virgin plastics use through design and production-related measures

Decisions taken at the design and manufacturing stage can restrain plastic demand and enhance circularity by increasing the durability and reparability of plastic products as well as by using recycled plastic or alternative materials in production. This stage forms the basis for the consumption and end-of-life treatment stage, as product design determines the way a plastic product is produced, and from which materials, how it is consumed and disposed of as well as whether it can be repaired, reused and remanufactured. These stages also include the sourcing of materials that are used to manufacture a product, as well as the production process itself. A number of policy instruments can help make product design and production of plastic products in Albania more circular. As these instruments are more challenging to implement, they are thus proposed to be introduced only in the medium to long term in Albania.

In the medium term, Albania should introduce eco-modulated fees for plastic packaging within the EPR take-back scheme for packaging that should be implemented in the short term (see Table 6.1 as well as Table 4.1 in Chapter 4). While in the short term the focus would be on increased recycling and material recovery through EPR take-back schemes, in the medium term it should be on using EPR take-back schemes to incentivise producers to design plastic products that are more circular. EPR take-back schemes can incentivise "design-for-environment" by making individual firms face the cost of waste management that is directly related to the characteristics of the products that they themselves have produced. The evidence suggests that this is often not the case in a collective producer responsibility organisation (PRO) scheme. In a collective PRO, a crucial policy choice, which underpins the effectiveness of the EPR, is the design of the fee governing firms' financial contributions to the PRO. Firms will only face clear incentives to reduce their end-of-life costs and improve the design of their products towards increased circularity if the fees that they have to pay to the PRO are "eco-modulated" (OECD, 2021[12]). Eco-modulated fees reflect the environmental characteristics of products that affect their end-of-life waste management costs (for example, recyclability and presence of hazardous substances) or even the entire product life cycle (for example, recycled content and product lifespan). For example, producer fees in Belgium for plastic packaging range from 0.1 EUR/kg for easy-to-recycle transparent colourless PET bottles to more than 1 EUR/kg for plastics which tend to be harder to recycle. First, in 2020, there were only three different tariffs for plastic packaging, ranging from 246 EUR/tonne to 711 EUR/tonne, but since 2022, nine different tariffs apply for plastic packaging. The lowest fee applies to transparent colourless PET bottles, which dropped significantly from 246 EUR/tonne in 2020 to 104 EUR/tonne in 2022. Conversely, the highest fees of more than 1 000 EUR/tonne apply to PE films and other plastic (OECD, 2023[2]). Albania could also start simply differentiating fees for reusable plastic packaging (no fee) and for single-use plastic packaging (price per tonne of material), as the Czech Republic did in the past (OECD, 2021[12]). The relative novelty of these policies means that there are only limited insights about the performance of these schemes.

To boost the use of recycled plastics, in the long term Albania will need to implement minimum plastics recycled content requirements for specific plastic waste streams, for example plastic packaging. Minimum recycled content mandates typically take the form of a regulatory requirement for producers of a certain type of product to use a minimum percentage of recycled material in their production. This could, for example, be a requirement to use a certain percentage minimum recycled content in the manufacture of plastic bottles. Requirements for recycled content are relatively rare but are increasingly discussed in the context of plastic waste management (IRP, 2020[13]). They can be imposed by direct regulation or can be applied indirectly, for example through a voluntary agreement, in the context of an environmental tax, an EPR system through eco-modulation or green public procurement (Box 6.3). For example, as mentioned above, the European Union has set targets in its EU Single-Use Plastics Directive to incorporate 25% of recycled plastic in the manufacture of PET bottles from 2025 and 30% in all plastic bottles from 2030. Minimum plastics recycled content requirements may also apply to other plastic packaging as well as products, such as carpets, textiles, print cartridges and plastic bags (OECD, forthcoming[14]).

To incentivise the use of secondary and recyclable plastics further and beyond the minimum recycled content requirements, Albania may consider taxes on virgin and non-recycled plastics in the long term. Taxes on plastics can be imposed at different points in the value chain, ranging from taxing polymers to taxing finished products containing plastics. For example, to date, the United Kingdom has implemented a national-level plastics packaging tax levied on plastic packaging with less than 30% recycled plastic content (in 2022) and Spain has a tax on non-reusable plastic packaging (since 2023). Taxes on plastics are also discussed in Chapter 4 and Section "2. Shifting demand from single-use plastics to alternatives and more reuse".

Box 6.3. Examples of how minimum recycled content requirements for plastics have been applied

As direct regulation

The EU Single-Use Plastics Directive requires plastic bottles to be made of at least 25% recycled content by 2025 and 30% recycled content by 2030.

Through a voluntary agreement

The Netherlands launched the Dutch Plastic Pact (Plastic Pact NL) in 2019 to make single-use plastic products and packaging more sustainable and suitable for reuse. This voluntary agreement includes four targets, one of which requires single-use plastic products to contain at least 35% of recycled plastic.

Within the context of a tax

Since 2022, the United Kingdom applies a tax (200 GBP/tonne) on plastic packaging with less than 30% recycled material.

In Italy, a series of fiscal incentives, mainly in the form of tax credits for enterprises, have been introduced to discourage the use of virgin materials and incentivise the use of recycled or compostable materials, among other plastics. These include tax credits for enterprises that apply to the purchase of products made out of recycled plastics; packaging containing recycled paper, plastics or aluminium; and biodegradable packaging (introduced via the 2019 Budget Law). Tax credits correspond to 36% of the expenses incurred by the enterprise, up to a maximum annual amount of EUR 20 000.

In an extended producer responsibility scheme through eco-modulation

Extended producer responsibility fees can be modulated in line with the share of recycled materials in the product to incentivise such design-for-environment. For example, products that verifiably meet thresholds for recycled content could receive a bonus resulting in a lowered fee. Some producer responsibility organisations have started to experiment with incentives to increase recycled content. For example, in France, a 50% fee reduction is provided for polyethylene and polypropylene packaging with at least 50% recycled content.

Sources: RIVM (2020[15]); HM Revenue & Customs (2020[16]); CITEO (2021[17]); Laubinger et al. (2021[18]).

Also in the long term, to address the plastic product design and production in general, Albania will need to support and scale up innovation into more recyclable plastic materials, plastics recycling technologies and processes (to the extent possible) as well as plastics reuse and reduction. Innovation (and R&D) can be promoted at every stage of the plastics life cycle, from the introduction of new materials in the production phase to new technologies for plastic waste sorting or recycling. Certain plastic products are made up of different types of plastic, which make them difficult to recycle. Providing funding for new recycling technologies is, therefore, crucial to improve plastic waste management and produce secondary plastic material that can be used as recycled content in products. R&D programmes can also focus on technologies to reduce microplastics emissions. Microplastics are highly relevant for the textiles industry as they often occur during use, such as from releases of microfibers when garments are washed. Innovation and R&D could be supported in Albania through already established programmes for scientific research activities through the National Agency for Scientific Research and Innovation and financing schemes offered by the Albanian Investment Development Agency and the Innovation Fund.

4. Cross-cutting measures

To support a transition to a more circular use of plastics, Albania should also implement two cross-cutting measures in the short and medium term.

First, in the short term, Albania will need to work on raising awareness and educating businesses, public authorities and households on plastic waste prevention, circular design and littering. Knowledge and capacity building includes a better understanding of the environmental impact of plastic waste generation, the benefits of reusing plastic products and favouring repair over buying new products, among others. Businesses need to be aware of circular economy solutions and the benefits these can bring. They should also understand the use and application of new circular business models (e.g. sharing schemes, reuse and repair centres). Consumers are more likely to comply with waste management regulation and respond to incentives if they have information on how to properly sort waste and a better understanding of how sorted waste is used for recycling. Information campaigns play an important role in ensuring the proper disposal of plastic waste, particularly because of the variety of polymers (OECD, 2023[2]). Some awareness-raising activities have been conducted in Albania, such as the 2019 EU campaign "Plastic leaves no space for life" about plastic pollution and alternatives to single-use plastics. Moreover, the awareness-raising campaign on waste management recently undertaken by the National Environmental Agency aims to reduce the generation of plastic waste, especially single-use plastic items and targets both citizens and public authorities. Municipalities also organise the "Let's do it" public awareness campaigns promoting waste reduction, reuse and recycling for all waste streams, including plastics. Awareness-raising and education can be improved by further developing information and training materials, designing campaigns, and sharing best practices through catalogues or online platforms. This is often carried out in co-operation with civil society organisations. Albania could also aim at mainstreaming the circular economy into education programmes in schools, vocational education and training, and higher education. It is recommended to develop circular modules for different levels of the education system (schools, vocational education and training, and higher education), and to support voluntary activities by students and schools.

Second, in the medium term, Albania could develop a strategy to curb plastic pollution, including marine plastic litter. Albania is involved in the Western Balkans regional co-operation programme on preventing of plastic pollution, including marine litter. To support the programme's objectives, Albania could develop a national strategy on plastic pollution, with a focus on marine litter, that would outline key strategic objectives and possibly targets as well as measures to achieve them. One aim of such a strategy could be to prevent litter from entering the marine and coastal environment, and to support its removal, so as to bring environmental, economic and social benefits. Some of the measures could focus on improving waste prevention, waste collection and management in coastal areas in general, promoting effective wastewater treatment and storm water management, raising awareness, supporting removal and remediation activity, and strengthening stakeholder engagement (OECD, 2019[19]). Better waste management systems allow plastic waste to be captured before it impacts the environment. This strategy would be also relevant to the tourism sector, as Albania is an important seaside tourist destination. In this regard, Croatian plastic waste reduction initiatives can offer good practice examples on the development of strategic documents and the implementation of measures to curb plastic pollution in important tourist destinations (Box 6.4). Albania could also support businesses in the tourism sector in implementing systems for plastic waste reduction and minimisation in their business operations and strategies (see Chapter 5).

Box 6.4. How Croatian cities and islands are moving to reduce plastic waste

Tourism is a major industry in Croatia, significantly contributing to waste generation and putting a substantial strain on local waste management systems. During Croatia's tourist peaks in summer, waste generation increases considerably in coastal municipalities, with tourists producing up to twice as much waste as residents. In 2018, waste produced by tourists accounted for 9% of total municipal waste generated in the country. In the city of Dubrovnik, for instance, it is estimated that municipal waste increases by up to 400% in the summer months due to the city's popularity.

Two initiatives were launched in 2020 to curb plastic pollution and reduce the plastic footprint in Croatian popular tourist destinations, implemented by the Association for Nature, Environment and Sustainable Development Sunce and funded by the Beyond Med Association and the Worldwide Fund for Nature:

- "Plastic Smart Cities Croatia" as part of which the city of Dubrovnik committed to reducing its plastic footprint by eliminating single-use plastics by 2030. As part of the project, an action plan to reduce plastic pollution was developed and adopted for the period 2021-26. It includes measures to improve the collection and disposal of compostable and biodegradable plastic waste and the establishment of a Reuse Center. It also includes the adoption of legal measures for limiting the use of disposable plastics by all public companies. Education and communication with the public are essential components of the action plan, with hospitality and tourism actors being important target groups in this regard.
- "For Plastic Free Croatian Islands", whose main objective is to implement waste management based on the principles of reduce, reuse and recycle in the islands of Dugi Otok and Hvar. A study was carried out to better understand the waste management system in place, the type of single-use plastic used and the level of plastic pollution. A "Plastic Free" Action Plan will then be developed in co-operation with identified stakeholders to propose alternatives for single-use plastics and increase awareness among the general public and businesses. The project also strives to build local, national and regional partnerships to encourage the sharing of experience and the replication of the actions implemented.

Sources: UNEP and WTTC (2021[20]); World Bank (2021[21]); Plastic Smart Cities (2021[22]).

References

Berlin Process Summit (2023), *Regional Joint Statement on Prevention of Plastic Pollution, Including Marine Litter*, https://www.berlinprocess.de/uploads/documents/regional-joint-statement-on-preventing-plastic-pollution-including-marine-litter-bp-summit-2023_1697614083.pdf. [3]

CITEO (2021), *Le Tarif 2021 pour le Recyclage des Emballages Ménagers*, CITEO, http://20210201_Citeo_Outil interactif_2021.pdf. [17]

Drab, J., M. Engel and T. Kristofory (2020), *Sorting Out Waste Sorting*, Institute for Environmental Policy, Ministry of Environment of the Slovak Republic, Bratislava, https://www.minzp.sk/files/iep/sorting_out_waste_sorting.pdf. [10]

Dráb, J. and S. Slučiaková (2018), *Real Price of Deposit*, Institute for Environmental Policy, Ministry of Environment of the Slovak Republic, Bratislava, https://www.minzp.sk/iep/publikacie/ekonomicke-analyzy/skutocna-cena-zalohy.html. [9]

EEA (2021), *Municipal Waste Management in Western Balkan Countries: Albania*, European Environment Agency, Copenhagen, https://www.eea.europa.eu/themes/waste/waste-management/municipal-waste-management-country/albania-municipal-waste-factsheet-2021/#:~:text=Albania%20has%20a%20new%20national,the%20treatment%20of%20residual%20MSW. [5]

EKO-KOM (n.d.), *EKO-KOM website*, https://www.ekokom.cz. [6]

HM Revenue & Customs (2020), "Plastic packaging tax", https://www.gov.uk/government/publications/introduction-of-plastic-packaging-tax/plastic-packaging-tax. [16]

IRP (2020), *Resource Efficiency and Climate Change: Material Efficiency Strategies for a Low-Carbon Future*, Hertwich, E., R. Lifset, S. Pauliuk, and N. Heeren, International Resource Panel, United Nations Environment Programme, Nairobi, https://www.resourcepanel.org/reports/resource-efficiency-and-climate-change (accessed on 11 May 2021). [13]

Laubinger, F. et al. (2021), "Modulated fees for Extended Producer Responsibility schemes (EPR)", *OECD Environment Working Papers*, No. 184, OECD Publishing, Paris, https://doi.org/10.1787/2a42f54b-en. [18]

Monier, V., M. Hestin and J. Cavé (2014), *Packaging Waste in the Czech Republic: Development of Guidance on Extended Producer Responsibility (EPR)*, European Union, Brussels. [8]

OECD (2024), *Material consumption* (indicator), https://doi.org/10.1787/84971620-en (accessed on 21 February 2024). [23]

OECD (2023), *Towards a National Circular Economy Strategy for Hungary*, OECD Publishing, Paris, https://doi.org/10.1787/1178c379-en. [2]

OECD (2022), *Global Plastics Outlook: Economic Drivers, Environmental Impacts and Policy Options*, OECD Publishing, Paris, https://doi.org/10.1787/de747aef-en. [1]

OECD (2021), "Towards a national strategic framework for the circular economy in the Czech Republic: Analysis and a proposed set of key elements", *OECD Environment Policy Papers*, No. 27, OECD Publishing, Paris, https://doi.org/10.1787/5d33734d-en. [12]

OECD (2019), *Improving Resource Efficency to Combat Marine Plastic Litter: Issues Brief*, OECD, Paris, https://www.oecd.org/g20/summits/osaka/OECD-G20-Paper-Resource-Efficiency-and-Marine-Plastics.pdf. [19]

OECD (2018), *OECD Environmental Performance Reviews: Czech Republic 2018*, OECD Environmental Performance Reviews, OECD Publishing, Paris, https://doi.org/10.1787/9789264300958-en. [7]

OECD (forthcoming), *New Aspects of EPR: Extending Producer Responsibility to Additional Product Groups and Challenges Throughout the Product Lifecycle*, OECD, Paris, forthcoming. [14]

Plastic Smart Cities (2021), *Action Plan to Reduce Plastic Pollution in the City of Dubrovnik 2021-2026*, Plastic Smart Cities, https://www.dubrovnik.hr/uploads/posts/14644/Action-Plan-to-reduce-the-plastic-pollution-in-the-City-of-Dubrovnik-2021.-2026..pdf. [22]

RIVM (2020), *First Results Plastic Pact Netherlands*, Ministry of Health, Welfare and Sport, The Hague, https://www.rivm.nl/en/news/first-results-plastic-pact-netherlands. [15]

UNEP and WTTC (2021), *Rethinking Single-use Plastic Products in Travel & Tourism: Impacts, Management Practices and Recommendations*, United Nations Environment Programme, Nairobi, https://wedocs.unep.org/bitstream/handle/20.500.11822/36324/RSUP.pdf. [20]

Watkins, E. et al. (2019), "Policy approaches to incentivise sustainable plastic design", *OECD Environment Working Papers*, No. 149, OECD Publishing, Paris, https://doi.org/10.1787/233ac351-en. [11]

World Bank (2021), *Croatia: Cost of Environmental Degradation*, World Bank, Washington, DC, https://documents1.worldbank.org/curated/en/929211613036393029/pdf/Croatia-Cost-of-Environmental-Degradation.pdf. [21]

World Bank (2020), *Realizing the Blue Economy Potential in Albania*, World Bank, Washington, DC, https://openknowledge.worldbank.org/server/api/core/bitstreams/0e31273d-a69e-523a-92ec-d49b483daa1c/content. [4]

Notes

[1] Fines for non-compliance span between EUR 4 200 and EUR 12 500 and can lead to the loss of operation permit for repeated violations.

[2] Under the polluter-pays principle, the polluter should bear the expenses of pollution prevention and control measures. It is a fundamental principle for cost allocation by public authorities in OECD countries.

7 Monitoring framework

This chapter proposes a monitoring framework featuring specific indicators for each recommendation developed for the three priority areas for Albania's Circular Economy Roadmap. This framework will help the effective implementation of the circular economy roadmap, and will be instrumental for evaluating progress towards strategic targets and goals for Albania's circular transition.

Defining key indicators and monitoring progress

Establishing a circular economy monitoring framework is crucial for assessing progress towards the targets and goals outlined in the roadmap over time and the circular economy transition in Albania more generally, using a set of indicators. This framework will assist Albanian policy makers in comprehending the country's performance on selected circular economy indicators and pinpoint areas that require further intervention. The monitoring process should also serve as the foundation for setting new long-term priorities for the circular economy (European Commission, 2023[1]) and offer feedback for strategy and planning development for various actors in the economy (Alaerts et al., 2019[2]). This aligns with the dual purpose of indicators: forward-looking to provide guidance and backward-looking to provide feedback and assess performance (Ekins et al., 2019[3]).

A circular economy monitoring framework can take a variety of forms, drawing upon an extensive array of existing indicators and those under development. Existing circular economy monitoring frameworks encompass a broader collection of relevant indicators, recognising the difficulty of capturing the circular economy through a single indicator due to its cross-cutting and wide-ranging definition. These monitoring frameworks can adopt the structure of a set of individual indicators, not necessarily linked, or they can be organised using a multi-tiered approach with a limited number of headline indicators (for communication purposes), complemented by a dashboard featuring specific thematic indicators. Employing a multi-layered approach allows for incorporating more detailed information at additional levels (e.g. regional, city, sectoral or product groups levels) or concerning specific strategic objectives and recommendations.

Academic literature strongly advocates moving beyond commonly used macro-level indicators to include indicators that offer direct feedback to policy makers on specific products and services, and that address consumer and business behaviour, as well as societal needs, related to the circular economy (Alaerts et al., 2019[2]; Ekins et al., 2019[3]; Giljum et al., 2011[4]; Potting et al., 2018[5]). Moreover, there is a need for supplementary indicators to precisely measure the effects and process of the transition itself, connecting the circular economy to environmental impacts while capturing possible rebound effects (Potting et al., 2018[5]; Alaerts et al., 2019[2]).

Two sets of indicators are proposed for Albania's monitoring framework

The proposed monitoring framework to support the implementation of the recommendations of the roadmap (Table 7.1) has a two-tier structure:

1. A set of headline indicators to monitor the economy-wide circular transition in Albania (Table 7.2). These indicators are largely based on the European Union's circular economy monitoring framework (Eurostat, 2023[6]) and are grouped into five categories: 1) production and consumption; 2) waste management; 3) secondary raw materials; 4) competitiveness and innovation; and 5) global sustainability and resilience.
2. Additionally, a set of indicators per priority area to monitor the progress made on specific recommendations (Table 7.3). Some of these indicators could be qualitative, for instance, certain operational indicators monitoring the progress made on a specific recommendation (e.g. the implementation has started, is ongoing or completed). Others are currently at an experimental stage, requiring further development of the indicator or additional data collection (e.g. monitoring the revenues generated from specific environmental taxes).

The proposed sets of indicators intend to provide a comprehensive overview of relevant indicators that can help monitor the implementation of the recommendations as well as Albania's overall circular economy transition. Albania may want to consider these all-encompassing lists of indicators during the preparation of the future policy framework or an action plan and select those for which data are or might become available. That said, to ensure effective and evidence-based policy making, data collection and co-ordination of the collection process should be improved, and existing gaps in the availability and quality of key circular economy-related data should be addressed, starting with those related to waste generation and waste management. Establishing an impact assessment mechanism is a potential solution to ensure that the monitoring framework is effectively executed and to secure its long-term continuity.

Table 7.1. Complete list of recommendations for each of the three priority areas

Priority area	Short term	Medium term	Long term
Economic instruments	Put in place planned extended producer responsibility (EPR) take-back schemes	Implement landfill taxes with discounts for good sorting/high recycling	Introduce EPR take-back schemes for new products (e.g. textiles)
	Reform household waste charges (introduce a gradual increase of waste charges with discounts for good waste management practices, promote low-cost pay-as-you-throw schemes and improve enforcement)	Gradually increase the (mandatory) use of green criteria as award criteria in public procurement	Consider introducing material taxes on extracted materials/plastics
	Introduce green public procurement, with a focus on priority sectors (capacity building, methodology guidelines)	Consider introducing a tourist tax to account for additional environmental costs related to tourism that are not covered by existing taxation schemes	Introduce minimum recycled content requirements within green public procurement (paper, plastics)
	Introduce reuse and recycling credit schemes that offer payments for the removal of items from municipal waste for recycling and reuse		Strengthen the use of tax relief for a circular economy (e.g. reduced value-added tax for eco-innovation, tax credits for food donations)
			Consider introducing incineration taxes
Circular business models for small and medium-sized enterprises	Provide awareness-raising campaigns and training programmes on the circular economy for small and medium-sized enterprises (SMEs), including showcasing good practices and access to finance	Continue facilitating the exchange of practices and learning from peers, including cross-sectoral knowledge development	Consider additional investment support for SMEs (e.g. accelerated depreciation rate, guarantee schemes, tax incentives)
	Introduce calls for circular business models projects within existing and new funding programmes	Provide support to SMEs on environmental legislation and obligations to ease their administrative burden	Organise investor-entrepreneur matchmaking events
	Provide financial, combined with technical, assistance to SMEs (business support, access to finance support)	Support capacity building and entrepreneurship skills as well as vocational training	
	Support collaboration between SMEs and academia, as well as regional and international collaboration on research and development and innovation		
	Establish a circular economy stakeholder/business platform to strengthen collaboration within and across value chains		
	Consider establishing a dedicated funding programme for SMEs to scale up circular business models		
Plastics, with a focus on marine litter	Improve municipal waste management in general	Introduce eco-modulated fees for plastic packaging within the EPR scheme for packaging	Support and scale up innovation into more recyclable plastic materials, plastics recycling technologies and processes as well as plastics reuse and reduction
	Improve separate collection of plastic waste and other packaging	Develop a strategy to curb plastic pollution, including marine plastic litter	Introduce minimum recycled content requirements for specific plastic waste streams
	Raise awareness and educate businesses, public authorities and households on plastic waste prevention, circular design and	Use green public procurement to favour reusable and recycled plastics	Consider taxes on virgin and non-recycled plastics

	littering		
	Implement an EPR take-back scheme for packaging (including plastic packaging)	Consider a deposit-refund system for plastic bottles	
	Introduce taxes and/or bans on certain single-use plastics		

Table 7.2. Proposed headline indicators based on the European Union's circular economy monitoring framework to monitor the economy-wide circular transition in Albania

No.	Indicator group	Name of the indicator
Production and consumption		
1	Material consumption	Material footprint (tonnes per capita)
2		Resource productivity (Index 2000=100)
3	Waste generation	Total waste generation per capita (kg per capita)
4		Generation of waste excluding major mineral wastes per gross domestic product (GDP) unit (kg per EUR 1 000, chain linked volumes [2010])
5		Generation of municipal waste per capita (kg per capita)
6		Food waste (kg per capita)
7		Generation of packaging waste per capita (kg per capita)
8		Generation of plastic packaging waste per capita (kg per capita)
Waste management		
9	Overall recycling rate	Recycling rate of municipal waste (%)
10		Recycling rate of all waste excluding major mineral waste (%)
11	Recycling rates for specific waste streams	Recycling rate of overall packaging waste (%)
12		Recycling rate of plastic packaging waste (%)
13		Recycling rate of waste from electrical and electronic equipment separately collected (%)
Secondary raw materials		
14	Contribution of recycled materials to raw materials demand	Circular material use rate (%)
15	Trade in recyclable raw materials	Imports (thousand tonnes)
16		Exports (thousand tonnes)
Competitiveness and innovation		
17	Private investment, jobs and gross value added related to circular economy sectors	Private investments (% of GDP at current prices)
18		Persons employed (% of total employment)
19		Gross value added (% of GDP at current prices)
20		Industrial symbiosis initiatives (number)
21	Innovation	Patents related to waste management and recycling (number)
Global sustainability and resilience		
23	Global sustainability from the circular economy	Greenhouse gas emissions from production activities (kg per capita)
24	Resilience from the circular economy	Material import dependency (%)

Sources: Eurostat (2023[6]); OECD (2021[7]).

Table 7.3. Proposed dashboard of specific indicators for the three priority areas

Indicator[1]	Description	Link to recommendation	Source[2]
Economic instruments			
Tax revenues or savings generated from circular economy-related tax instruments	Amount (ALL)	**Applies to all recommendations concerning tax instruments**	Data to be provided by the Ministry of Finance and Economy
Recovery rate of packaging waste	Ratio of overall packaging waste prepared for reuse, recycled or subject to material recovery to packaging waste generated (%)	**Effectively implement planned extended producer responsibility (EPR) take-back schemes**	Data to be provided by the Institute of Statistics (INSTAT)/National Environment Agency
Establishment of a Special Fund for Circular Economy[3]	Action-specific indicator for monitoring the creation of the fund (yes/no)		Data to be provided by the Ministry of Tourism and Environment/ Ministry of Finance and Economy
Share of income distributed to the Special Fund for Circular Economy[3]	Income raised from the fund for the fulfilment of the EPR Law (%, ALL)		Data to be provided by the Ministry of Tourism and Environment/ Ministry of Finance and Economy
Establishment of a programme for supporting reuse and recycling credit schemes	Action-specific indicator for monitoring the creation of the programme (yes/no)	**Introduce reuse and recycling credit schemes that would offer payments for the removal of items from municipal waste for recycling and reuse**	Data to be provided by the Ministry of Finance; municipal authorities
Illegal landfills	Change in the number of illegal landfills, amount of illegally discarded municipal waste (m^3)		INSTAT
Landfill tax proceeds	Amount (ALL)	**Implement landfill tax discounts for good sorting/high recycling**	Data to be provided by the Ministry of Finance and Economy
Waste collection coverage	Share of households that have access to a reliable waste collection service	**Reform household waste charges (introduce a gradual increase of waste charges with discounts for good waste management practices, promote low-cost pay-as-you-throw schemes and improve enforcement)**	Data to be provided by the Ministry of Tourism and Environment; municipal authorities
Campaigns to raise public awareness on waste charges	Action-specific indicator monitoring the implementation of comprehensive, culturally appropriate public education and awareness-raising initiatives		Data to be provided by the Ministry of Tourism and Environment; municipal authorities
Waste generation	Generation of municipal waste per capita (kg per capita); generation of waste excluding major mineral wastes per GDP unit (kg per EUR 1 000, chain linked volumes [2010])		INSTAT
Separate collection	Share of municipal waste collected separately compared to all municipal waste generated (%); separate collection of paper, metal, plastic and glass		INSTAT
Uptake of home composting	Measures the extent of home composting		Indicators to be developed, data to be collected by municipal authorities, would require specific surveys
Tax proceeds earmarked to cover environmental and infrastructure costs during tourism peaks	Share of tax revenue that covers increased costs in various environmental fields (e.g. water, waste, etc.)	**Consider introducing a tourist tax to account for additional environmental costs related to tourism that are not covered by existing taxation schemes**	Data to be provided by municipal authorities
Domestic extraction of raw material	Thousand tonnes	**Consider introducing material taxes on extracted materials/plastics**	INSTAT
Domestic material consumption of raw material	Amount of virgin material directly used by the economy (thousand tonnes)		INSTAT

<table>
<tr><td>Green public procurement</td><td>Green public procurement share in public contracts (in volume and value) across all procured products and services (%)</td><td>Introduce green public procurement, with a focus on priority sectors (capacity building, methodology guidelines)</td><td>Data to be provided by the Public Procurement Office</td></tr>
<tr><td>Products/services covered by minimum recycled content criteria in green public procurement</td><td>Number</td><td>Introduce minimum recycled content requirements within green public procurement (paper, plastics)</td><td>Data to be provided by the Public Procurement Office</td></tr>
<tr><td colspan="4">Circular business models for small and medium-sized enterprises (SMEs)</td></tr>
<tr><td>Budget allocated to circular economy projects under a concrete programme</td><td>Amount (ALL)</td><td rowspan="4">Introduce calls for circular business model projects within existing and new funding programmes that provide grants and soft loans. The financial support in the form of grants and loans should be combined with technical and other assistance to SMEs</td><td>Data to be provided by the Albanian Investment Development Agency (AIDA)</td></tr>
<tr><td>Training courses on circular business models</td><td>Number of events organised; number of technical modules created as part of funding programmes</td><td>AIDA</td></tr>
<tr><td>SMEs benefitting from financial support for the creation of new circular business models</td><td>Number of SMEs</td><td>AIDA</td></tr>
<tr><td>SMEs benefitting from non-financial support for the creation of new circular business models</td><td>Number of SMEs</td><td>AIDA</td></tr>
<tr><td>SMEs supported by funding programmes to scale up circular business models</td><td>Number of SMEs</td><td>Consider establishing a dedicated funding programme for SMEs to scale up circular business models</td><td>AIDA</td></tr>
<tr><td>Creation of a circular economy platform[4]</td><td>Action-specific indicator for monitoring the creation of the platform (yes/no)</td><td rowspan="3">Establish a circular economy stakeholder/business platform to strengthen collaboration, information exchange and exchange of good practices[2]</td><td>Data to be provided by the co-ordinating institution (e.g. Ministry of Tourism and Environment)</td></tr>
<tr><td>Number of platform members[4]</td><td>Number</td><td>Data to be provided by the co-ordinating institution (e.g. Ministry of Tourism and Environment)</td></tr>
<tr><td>Number of events/workshops organised as part of the platform[4]</td><td>Number</td><td>Data to be provided by the co-ordinating institution (e.g. Ministry of Tourism and Environment)</td></tr>
<tr><td>Environment-related R&D and innovation expenditure by state and business sectors</td><td>Gross expenditure on research and development (GERD) (%)</td><td>Support collaboration between SMEs and academia, as well as regional and international collaboration on R&D and innovation</td><td>Indicator to be developed based on Eurostat by the Agency for Research, Technology and Innovation. Data to be provided by the National Agency for Scientific Research and Innovation or AIDA</td></tr>
<tr><td>Matchmaking events organised</td><td>Number of events</td><td>Organise investor-entrepreneur matchmaking events</td><td>AIDA</td></tr>
<tr><td>Awareness-raising campaigns on the circular economy</td><td>Number of campaigns</td><td rowspan="2">Raise awareness on the circular economy and circular business models for SMEs through additional communication campaigns and training programmes, including showcasing of good practices and access-to-finance possibilities</td><td>Data to be provided by AIDA, chambers of commerce and industry</td></tr>
<tr><td>Awareness of SMEs on circular business models</td><td>Share of SMEs aware of the circular economy</td><td>Regional Cooperation Council (Balkan Barometer Survey) or nationwide survey</td></tr>
<tr><td>Awareness campaigns to reduce</td><td>Number of campaigns;</td><td>Continue facilitating the</td><td>Data to be provided by the</td></tr>
</table>

food waste in the tourism sector	number of restaurants/hotels involved	**exchange of practices and peer learning, including cross-sectoral knowledge development**	Ministry of Tourism and Environment
Awareness campaigns to reduce textile waste	Number of campaigns; number of businesses involved		Data to be provided by AIDA or the Ministry of Finance and Economy
Mainstreaming education for the circular economy into university-level curricula	Action-specific indicator for monitoring the implementation of the recommendation (yes/no)	**Support capacity building and entrepreneurship skills as well as vocational training on the circular economy**	Data to be provided by the Ministry of Education and Sports
		Plastics	
Introduction of EPR schemes planned by law	Action-specific indicator for monitoring the implementation of EPR schemes	**Improve waste management in general: separate collection of plastic (and other packaging) waste and implement an EPR take-back scheme for packaging, including plastic packaging**	Data to be provided by the Ministry of Tourism and Environment
Collection facilities installed	Number of collection facilities installed	**Consider introducing a deposit-refund system for plastic bottles**	Data to be provided by the Ministry of Tourism and Environment
Collection of plastic bottles	Share of separate collection of plastic bottles of all single-use bottles placed on the market (%)		
Introduction of a ban on all single-use plastic bags (full alignment with the EU Single-Use Plastics Directive)	Action-specific indicator for monitoring the introduction of the ban (yes/no)	**Introduce taxes and/or bans on certain single-use plastic products**	Data to be provided by the Ministry of Tourism and Environment
Eco-modulated fees within EPR for packaging	Action-specific indicator for monitoring the introduction of the fees (yes/no)	**Introduce eco-modulated fees for plastic packaging**	Data to be provided by Ministry of Tourism and Environment
Funding and training for new recycling technologies	Number of programmes for innovation and R&D activities in the field of plastics	**Support and scale up innovation into more recyclable plastics materials, plastics recycling technologies and processes**	Data to be provided by the National Agency for Scientific Research and Innovation, AIDA, Innovation Fund
Public expenditure on R&D related to plastics recycling	Amount (ALL)		Data to be provided by the National Agency for Scientific Research and Innovation
Awareness-raising activities carried out for plastic use reduction, reuse and recycling targeting businesses	Number of activities	**Raise awareness and educate businesses, public authorities and households on plastic waste prevention, circular design and littering (campaigns, catalogues, online platforms; mainstreaming the circular economy into education programmes in schools)**	Data to be provided by the Ministry of Tourism and Environment
Public awareness raising and education campaign on plastic waste and marine litter	Number of campaigns		Data to be provided by the Ministry of Tourism and Environment
Municipal or regional web catalogues or platforms for information on plastic waste prevention	Number of established platforms; number of materials and resources accessible on line; level of traffic on the web platform		Data to be provided by regional or municipal authorities
Circular economy in the educational system	Number of students educated/trained on circular economy fields of activity; number of events organised in relation to pedagogical circular economy activities		Data to be provided by the Ministry of Education, Sports and Youth
Strategy with all the necessary elements adopted (timeline, budget, responsible institution, consultation process)	Action-specific indicator for monitoring the adoption of the strategy (yes/no)	**Develop a strategy to curb plastic pollution, including marine plastic litter**	Data to be provided by the Ministry of Tourism and Environment

1. Headline indicators outlined in Table 7.2 serve as the main benchmarks for monitoring progress in the implementation of the proposed recommendations. The indicators outlined in this table are complementary to those, capturing additional implementation aspects.
2. The source column refers to institutions already collecting relevant data or those that could be in charge of collecting such data in the future.

3. The establishment of the Special Fund for Circular Economy is a measure envisaged as part of the draft Extended Producer Responsibility Law, under public consultation at the time of drafting, and is hence subject to change.
4. Circular economy stakeholders' platform-related indicators might differ depending on the format of the platform (on line, physical, hybrid).
Note: ALL: Albanian lek.

References

Alaerts, L. et al. (2019), "Towards a more direct policy feedback in circular economy monitoring via a societal needs perspective", *Resources, Conservation and Recycling*, Vol. 149, pp. 363-371, https://doi.org/10.1016/j.resconrec.2019.06.004. [2]

Ekins, P. et al. (2019), "The circular economy: What, why, how and where", Background paper for an OECD/EC Workshop on 5 July 2019, https://www.oecd.org/cfe/regionaldevelopment/Ekins-2019-Circular-Economy-What-Why-How-Where.pdf. [3]

European Commission (2023), *Communication on a Revised Monitoring Framework for the Circular Economy*, European Commission, Brussels, https://eur-lex.europa.eu/legal-content/EN/TXT/?uri=COM%3A2023%3A306%3AFIN&qid=1684143860344. [1]

Eurostat (2023), "Circular Economy Monitoring Framework", https://ec.europa.eu/eurostat/web/circular-economy/monitoring-framework (accessed on 27 November 2023). [6]

Giljum, S. et al. (2011), "A comprehensive set of resource use indicators from the micro to the macro level", *Resources, Conservation and Recycling*, Vol. 55/3, pp. 300-308, https://doi.org/10.1016/j.resconrec.2010.09.009. [4]

OECD (2021), *The OECD Inventory of Circular Economy indicators*, OECD, Paris, https://www.oecd.org/cfe/cities/InventoryCircularEconomyIndicators.pdf. [7]

Potting, J. et al. (2018), *Circular Economy: What We Want to Know and Can Measure – Framework and Baseline Assessment for Monitoring the Progress of the Circular Economy in the Netherlands*, PBL Netherlands Environmental Assessment Agency, The Hague, https://www.pbl.nl/sites/default/files/downloads/pbl-2018-circular-economy-what-we-want-to-know-and-can-measure-3217.pdf. [5]

Annex A. Stakeholder engagement in developing the Circular Economy Roadmap of Albania

Transitioning to a circular economy is a long-term process requiring broad societal consensus. This roadmap was developed through a multi-step process involving a wide range of stakeholders in a continuous dialogue spanning several months. This annex describes how the roadmap was designed.

Establishment of the circular economy co-ordination mechanism

As part of the inception phase of the “Supporting Green Transition through Circular Economy Roadmaps”, the OECD contacted its existing contacts in respective ministries responsible for the green economy, inviting them to identify a circular economy (CE) co-ordinator.

The OECD held meetings with the newly nominated CE co-ordinator and his team. During the discussions, the Ministry of Tourism and Environment and the OECD agreed to form a CE working group and to maintain a broader CE stakeholder platform to steer the roadmap design process and ensure that all parts of society were involved in the CE transition (Table A.1). To support the establishment of the working group and the CE platform, the OECD provided an initial list of relevant stakeholders from all parts of society to ensure an inclusive process: government institutions, international organisations (locally present and those working on the circular economy in Albania), academia, civil society and the private sector. Additional members suggested by the co-ordinating ministry completed the list and became members of the working group and the CE stakeholder platform.

In addition to the Albania-specific CE platform, the OECD established a Regional Circular Economy Peer Dialogue platform at the regional kick-off event in Istanbul, consisting of the CE co-ordinators from all six Western Balkan economies and representatives from their respective CE working groups, supported by the OECD/EU member countries (e.g. Hungary, Italy and Türkiye). Participants endorsed the regional platform, whose objective is to facilitate bilateral and multilateral exchange, peer learning, and policy dialogue on circular economy transition efforts in the Western Balkans and beyond. Members of the platform contributed to the development of the Circular Economy Roadmap of Albania by sharing their feedback and lessons learnt in the design of their respective CE roadmaps in different phases of the development process (e.g. prioritisation exercise, drafting).

Table A.1. Stakeholders engaged in the Albanian Circular Economy Platform

Government institutions	International community	Civil society organisations	Academia	Private sector
Ministry of Tourism and Environment (lead ministry)	European Union Delegation	Albanian Green Institute	Agriculture University of Tirana	Union of Chambers of Commerce and Industry
Ministry of Finance and Economy	Deutsche Gesellschaft für Internationale Zusammenarbeit (GIZ)	Build Green Group	Beder University	Albanian E-commerce Association
Ministry of Infrastructure and Energy	French Development Agency	Center for Competitive Skills	Polytechnic University of Tirana, Faculty of Civil Engineering	Albania Invest
Ministry of Foreign Affairs	United Nations Development Programme (UNDP)	Circular Economy Club – Tirana	University of Tirana, Faculty of Economy	Albanian Manufacturers Union
Albanian Investment Development Agency	United Nations Industrial Development Organization	Cooperation and Development Institute	University of Tirana, Faculty of Natural Sciences	ICC Albania
Institute of Statistics		Environmental Center for Development Education and Networking	Urban Research Institute	Pro-export – Albanian association for textile and footwear
National Environment Agency		Environmental & Territorial Management Institute		
Public Procurement Office		GO2 Albania – Sustainable Urban Planning Organization		
Ministry of Local Government		Institute for Environmental Policy		
		Milieukontakt		
		Qarkon Platform		
		The Door		

Kick-start meeting with key circular economy stakeholders in Albania

After the establishment of the CE co-ordination mechanism, in collaboration with the CE co-ordinator, the OECD facilitated several stakeholder meetings to officially establish the CE platform and gather initial takeaways on the circular economy. The main objectives of these meetings were to clarify the roles of members of the platform, collect data and information on the development of strategic circular economy documents and activities, and consult stakeholders on economy-specific aspects to be considered during the drafting of the roadmap. During these meetings, the OECD presented the main pillars, objectives and timeline for the project while outlining the steps to be taken to support the design and implementation of the roadmap. The CE co-ordinator informed participants about CE government initiatives and priorities and moderated the discussion with the CE stakeholders. The OECD also liaised with locally present international actors (e.g. UNDP, GIZ) working on CE-related projects to create synergies and avoid any duplication of efforts in driving Albania's circular economy transition.

Further to the stakeholders' meetings, the CE co-ordinator established the CE working group of Albania, made up of representatives of the key CE-related government and non-governmental institutions.

Identifying the state-of-play of the circular economy in Albania

The first step in designing Albania's Circular Economy Roadmap was identifying the state-of-play of the circular economy in the country. The diagnostic built on the latest findings of the OECD *Competitiveness*

Outlook 2021 ("Environmental policy" chapter) and the OECD *SME Policy Index 2022* ("SMEs in a green economy" chapter) and was complemented by extensive research. In particular, the OECD conducted a literature review of relevant policies, strategies and laws in Albania; desk research on OECD and other renowned institutions' reports covering circular economy trends in Albania; an analysis of circular economy strategic documents and roadmaps in other OECD countries; and compiled statistical data. The diagnostic was further enriched with the feedback obtained during the stakeholders' meetings.

The diagnostic maps all CE-relevant policy and regulatory frameworks in Albania and outlines key economic features, recent circular economy and environmental trends, ongoing initiatives and projects, critical sectors, and horizontal policy areas for addressing the barriers to a circular economy.

Throughout the drafting process, CE working group members provided written comments, feedback and any additional information that would enhance the analytical depth and comprehensiveness of the mapping documents. In addition, the OECD held a virtual meeting with the Albanian CE working group to discuss the draft document and fill in remaining data gaps on the status quo of the circular economy in Albania.

Reaching consensus on priority areas for the Circular Economy Roadmap of Albania

The OECD presented a total of ten pre-selected priority areas to the Albanian working group at a prioritisation meeting in September 2023 in Tirana, explaining the rationale and providing a set of preliminary recommendations set over the short, medium and long term. Lively discussions revealed a tentative preview of priorities and were enriched further by first-hand insights from experiences presented by experts from OECD countries – members of the Regional Circular Economy Peer Dialogue platform (namely Hungary and Italy).

Based on this, in a follow up meeting, the working group members selected three areas for the Circular Economy Roadmap of Albania.

Wide consultations on the draft Circular Economy Roadmap and publishing

The OECD developed detailed policy recommendations for each of the priority areas selected by the working group, which were accompanied by good practice examples. The OECD shared the draft roadmap with all members of the working group for review and comment. The draft was also sent for consultations to a wider group of stakeholders, including international community representatives, the European Commission and the members of the Regional CE Peer Dialogue platform. Before its publication in Q1 2024, the roadmap was validated by the Editorial Board of the OECD Global Relations and Co-operation Directorate.

Annex B. Development co-operation projects on the circular economy in Albania

Table B.1. International development co-operation projects on the circular economy in Albania

Organisation	Project title	Project details	Budget
Swiss Agency for Development and Cooperation)	Solid Waste Management in Berat – Phase II (2021-2026)	Integrated Solid Waste Management Programme (in partnership with the KfW). Further develop sustainable and climate-friendly solid waste management services in Albania. Planned to be the biggest waste programme in the country, covering at least half the territory.	Swiss budget: CHF 9 651 104 (EUR 10 018 084) Budget inclusive project partner: CHF 73 577 820 (EUR 76 375 591)
European Union (IPA III – Instrument for Pre-Accession Assistance)	EU 4 Circular Economy and Green Growth programme in Albania (2023)	The project's objective is to improve environmental protection and foster a circular economy and sustainable green growth in Albania. Different components are given in the four rows below (GIZ, AFD, UBA).	EUR 30.9 million
1. Deutsche Gesellschaft für Internationale Zusammenarbeit (GIZ)	EU 4 Circular Economy and Green Growth (2023-2027)	The technical assistance component, which includes: • a feasibility study on hazardous waste • waste prevention activities • support for extended producer responsibility – implementation for packaging waste and e-waste • data management. Fifteen municipalities have been selected to implement circular economy initiatives.	EUR 14.6 million
2. Deutsche Gesellschaft für Internationale Zusammenarbeit (GIZ)	EU 4 Circular Economy and Green Growth (2023-2027)	Implementation of the forthcoming Gender Agenda on Circular Economy (with a focus on the waste sector) prepared under the EU4Circular Economy and the Circular Economy for Sustainable Urban Development project. It aims to: • facilitate the collection of gender-disaggregated data and gender-sensitive policies • support women's entrepreneurship within the circular economy.	TBD
3. French Development Agency (AFD)	EU 4 Circular Economy and Green Growth (2023-TBC)	The component on the construction of landfills in municipalities in the Kukës and Gjirokastra/South Vlora	EUR 19 million (EU grant)

Donor	Project	Description	Budget
		regions, includes activities to: • increase recycling and reduce waste volumes • establish European Union (EU)-compliant landfills and waste facilities • assist Albanian authorities in further aligning Albania's solid waste management with EU standards. Investments will materialise from 2024-25 over a four-year period.	
4. Environment Agency Austria (UBA)	EU 4 Green project (2022-2025)	Aims to help the Western Balkans move towards a sustainable, climate-resilient future by enhancing the region's Green Agenda governance and tackling environmental challenges in line with EU accession. The project team, working with regional partners, is building implementation strategies and focusing on enhancing monitoring and reporting. Furthermore, a regional office has been set up in Albania. On the circular economy, the focus is on the local level in Albania, aimed at training municipal staff in practical circular economy measures.	EUR 11 million *Of which EUR 10 million from the European Union and EUR 1 million from the Austrian Development Agency*
GIZ	Modernized, Climate-friendly Solid Waste and Recycling Management in Albania (2020-2023)	Focuses on: • an improved data management system, inspection and regulation processes • recovery and trade in secondary resources and treatment of special waste • upgrading/rehabilitating six existing waste disposal sites.	EUR 1.2 million
GIZ	Integrated Waste Management and Marine Litter Prevention in the Western Balkans (2022-2025)	Regional project covering Albania, Bosnia and Herzegovina, Kosovo, and Montenegro. Supports partners to improve the implementation of co-ordinated strategies and approaches to reduce marine litter. Promotes co-ordination processes between governmental and non-governmental actors at the regional, national and local levels.	*Not available*
United Nations Development Programme	Support Albania's obligations under the United Nations Framework Convention on Climate Change (2016-2022)	Assists Albania in the preparation and submission of its First Biennial Update Report and its Fourth National Communication to the United Nations Framework Convention on Climate Change. Assists the Ministry of Tourism and Environment to revise the country's Nationally Determined Contribution	USD 1 080 097 (EUR 1 million)

		(NDC). The main scope is: the recalculation of the NDC baseline, under which updated data and new information will be provided; adding of new sectors with regards to climate change mitigation, i.e. agriculture, forestry and land use; and informing on climate change adaptation in the tourism, settlements and population sectors along the coast of Albania.	
United Nations Environment Programme	Strengthening Sound Chemicals and Pharmaceutical Waste Management (2019-2022)	Strengthened the institutional framework and national capacity of key stakeholders in Albania to address issues relating to waste and chemical management. Focused on pharmaceutical waste and obsolete chemicals by strengthening the capacity of the National Agency for Medicines & Medical Devices as the lead government agency for the management of pharmaceutical products and medical devices and strengthening the existing structure in the Ministry of Tourism and Environment (Chemical and Waste Office).	USD 318 789 (EUR 288 280)
United Nations Industrial Development Organization	Country Programme for Inclusive and Sustainable Industrial Development (2020-2024)	Aims to strengthen the government's effort towards sustainable and inclusive growth through 20 project proposals in 3 priority areas, one of which is sustainable energy for productive uses and environmental management. Some projects aim to boost the circular economy, such as through the development of eco-industrial parks.	*To be defined with donors*
World Bank	Country Partnership Framework for Albania (2023-2027)	The objective is to: strengthen the resilience of the government sector and households; strengthen the energy market framework and scale up renewable energy and energy efficiency; and protect the environment and reduce the country's carbon footprint. The umbrella project consists of four sub-projects, one of which is the Climate Resilience and Agriculture Development Project. This project aims to increase competitiveness and climate resilience of priority agri-food value chains by focusing on improving innovation in agriculture, enhancing smart irrigation, and access to local and EU markets.	USD 900 million (EUR 837 million) *indicative*

Notes: TBC: to be confirmed. The list is non-exhaustive.

Annex C. Non-governmental stakeholders involved in circular economy initiatives in Albania

Table C.1. Non-governmental organisations relevant to the circular economy transition in Albania

Organisation	Activities
Albanian Green Institute	• Its mission is to promote green thinking and actions in all political, economic, social and environmental aspects as well as greater commitment from civil society and citizens to the development of democracy in Albania and the implementation of green policies.
Build Green Group	• Research and development studies in different environment-related fields as well as research and implementation of short-, medium- and long-term sustainable development projects in various entities. • Published three mapping reports on the circular economy in the region, one of which was published in July 2023, underpinning the policy measures undertaken by the six Western Balkan economies, based on the European Union (EU) policy indicator set. • Established the LogEx Community in December 2021, a partnership between universities, civil society organisations, academia and business actors from the six Western Balkan economies as well as the region's diaspora, with a focus on the intersection between the circular economy, innovation and the labour market. LogEx marked its second year of existence with a circular economy week in the region with joint activities in each economy. • Released a report in June 2023 mapping circular economy activities based on the type of industry in Albania. The report was followed by an online open platform where all circular businesses in all Western Balkan economies can showcase their work and their level of circularity.
Center for Competitive Skills	• Implemented a project in 2020 on raising the awareness of civil society organisations, small and medium-sized enterprises, and the educational system regarding the importance of the circular economy. • Established "Qarkonomia" in 2020, a platform to raise awareness on the circular economy in Albania.
Circular Economy Club Tirana	• Network of experts, academics and entrepreneurs to support the circular economy transition in the capital city.
Co-PLAN Institute for Habitat Development	• Organised a regional conference on the circular economy in 2020 focusing on circular opportunities and challenges and municipalities' role in further promoting the circular model.
Environmental Center for Development Education and Networking	• Led a programme in 2019 supported by the European Union to raise awareness on the concept of a circular economy, through content classes with students and training with civil society organisations and businesses interested in the topic. • A series of activities took place in 2020 to promote practical model approaches in Albanian cities, including a two-day workshop in Tirana.
Environmental & Territorial Management Institute	• Promotes environmental and territorial management at the regional, national and international levels. • Working on a project highlighting the main challenges hampering the transition to a circular economy.
GO2 Albania	• Sustainable urban planning, with a specific focus on natural environments, sustainable transport and sustainable tourism.
Institute for Environmental Policy	• Promotes increasing environmental sustainability in Albania through policies, projects, programmes, awareness, public actions and campaigns in the field of environment. • Implemented a project on the circular economy through organic waste composting in Baldushk (2021-23) through funding from the Swedish International Development Cooperation Agency.
Milieukontakt	• Experience in implementing projects in waste management, mostly though the support of local governments.
Urban Research Institute	• Conducts several projects on environmental protection and eco-tourism, such as on marine litter management. • Extended expertise on waste management issues in Albania; its projects include introducing EU standards on recycling and building structures with recycled materials.

Note: The list is non-exhaustive.

Table C.2. Academia relevant to the circular economy in Albania

Agricultural University of Tirana	• Centre for studies, scientific research, training and extension in the area of agriculture and food (agronomy, horticulture and plant protection, agribusiness, economy and agrarian policy, agro-environment and ecology, agro-food technology, aquaculture and fishery management, forestry engineering).
Polytechnic University of Tirana, Department of Environmental Engineering	• Organises plenary sessions on the circular economy, such as "The Circular Economy in the Wastewater Context".
Polytechnic University of Tirana, Faculty of Civil Engineering	• Co-organised a first of its kind workshop in Albania on wastewater management in the context of the circular economy.
University of Tirana, Faculty of Economy	• Held an international conference in 2022 bringing together scientists, researchers, practitioners and policy makers in partnership with other European academic stakeholders.
University of Tirana, Sustainable Development of Blue Economies	• Participating partner in the project "Sustainable Development of Blue Economies through Higher Education and Innovation in Western Balkan Countries".
Polis University, Faculty of Planning, Environment and Urban Management	• Programmes on environmental studies (Bsc) and environmental urban management (Msc) include courses on environmental economics, with a focus on the circular economy. • Organises workshops and conferences in partnership with the non-governmental organisation Co-PLAN on the circular economy.
Polytechnic University of Tirana, Textile Department	• Collaborates with the Albanian textile industry through technology transfer activities, such as workshops, seminars and conferences. • Undertakes projects to support quality management and improving materials resources in the textile industry.

Note: The list is non-exhaustive.

Table C.3. Private sector organisations relevant to the circular economy in Albania

Albanian E-commerce Association	• Supports Albanian companies in increasing online trading capacities by improving the service offered and increasing consumers' confidence in the safety of e-commerce.
Albanian Manufacturers Union	• Increases competitiveness through the promotion of digitalisation, innovation and the circular economy. • Organises workshops, such as increasing civil society's awareness of the circular economy.
Pro-export – Albanian association for textile and footwear	• Protects the interests of members of the association in relation to unfair competition, unifying efforts to create an environment conducive to the development of textile confectionery business. • Advocacy with government authorities.
Union or Chambers of Commerce and Industry	• Participated in a panel on Unlocking the Potential of the Circular Economy for Businesses in the Western Balkans: Opportunities, Barriers, and Good Practices organised by the Regional Cooperation Council and supported by the European Union.

Note: The list is non-exhaustive.

Table C.4. Companies with circular economy business models in Albania

Aiba Company	• Cattle food production company reusing its waste to produce soil fertilisers to be sold to farmers. The company is also investing in creating a new system that will make drying waste possible.
AZ Group Shpk	• The group is composed of three companies: 1) I.N.C.A. shpk, which is the only natural casing manufacturing company in Albania collecting and processing the natural casings from Albanian slaughterhouses; 2) PetEat shpk, which produces natural dog chews derived by animal products; and 3) AZ Rendering, which processes the organic waste from I.N.C.A. and PetEat, and collects and processes all of the industrial waste that could not be processed by the first two companies.
City Tex	• Garment factory – social business based on circular economy concepts.
Design By Pana	• Offers a variety of products ranging from home and restaurant to office furniture, entirely made of reused wood, mainly coming from old furniture and used wood pallets.
Eco Bag	• One of a few manufacturers and exporters of shopping bags in Albania. The shopping bags produced have a positive impact on the environment.
Everest IE	• Production of flexible plastic packaging, as industrial packaging and several food or non-food products. • The production is ISO 9001 certified for quality standards and ISO 14001 certified for complying with the environmental standards.

GER.ARD Company	• Offers recycling services of vehicle parts and electronic devices, the majority of which is exported to European Union countries.
GPR Albania	• Polymeren General Recycling Albania is one of the main recycling companies in Albania of plastic polymers, which are recycled using a modern and sophisticated German technology. • Its next investment will enable the transformation of current products from flex into granulate.
Green Recycling Albania	• Helps customers manage wastepaper and other waste materials through best-in-class services and solutions while safeguarding the environment and human health, and complying with the relevant legislation. • Produces a green report every year for each client measuring their contribution through waste collection and recycling services in reducing CO_2 emissions and saving energy, trees, water and landfill space.
IB Recycling	• Offers recycling of electrical and electronic scrap waste, processing and recycling of car exhausts, and many other electronic car and computer parts. Various car parts are recycled efficiently in one of the most modern facilities in place for recycling these products. • Focuses on ensuring the complete recycling of various car parts to turn them into manufacturing materials. Processes electronic scrap and all waste electronic equipment.
Immortelle Tirane	• Provides quality saplings and seeds of medicinal and aromatic plants. • Plans to provide necessary training from planting to harvesting. The goal is to increase organic farming, which will bring sustainable income to rural households and have a positive impact on the environment, as it will enable the regeneration of natural resources damaged by wild plant harvest. • Winner of the Partners Albania Green Ideas National Competition.
Inca Casing	• Involved in the full cycle of works related to processing, packaging and logistics of animal intestines and by-products.
Mobike	• Mobile app for bike rentals and sharing that started in 2018 in the municipality of Tirana (public-private partnership).
Organic Soap Roskovec	• Project initiated by the European Union aimed at refining organic waste from olive oil production into organic soap.
Pastrimi Detar	• Marine cleaning company dealing with port services; the collection, manipulation and burning of garbage from local and foreign ships; and the collection and processing of hydrocarbon waste from local and foreign ships and various entities that have oily waste (hydrocarbons).
Pemla	• Supports the green economy by promoting organic agriculture practices. Produces artisanal nut butters and other products using regionally cultivated ingredients and slow food processing techniques. • Composts or upcycles waste streams from food processing and uses exclusively reusable/recyclable or biodegradable packaging.
RecycAl	• Waste management company, dedicated to establishing Albania's first Circular Economy Park, featuring a substantial recycling zone, a facility for repairing and repurposing goods, and a compact educational centre to promote and exhibit circular economy concepts.
Permeti's Yummy Treasures	• Sells organic products: supports farmers, producers and housewives by selling their products. • The goal is to maximise the experience of tourists and visitors in Permeti by providing organic gastronomy and agro-tourism. • Winner of the Partners Albania Green Ideas National Competition.
Remix Toys	• Produces simple and unique toys made from recyclable materials.
Shtëpia e ofertave (Offers House)	• Network of shops that sell a variety of used products, mainly furniture, clothing, household appliances and sports accessories.

Note: The list is non-exhaustive.

www.ingramcontent.com/pod-product-compliance
Lightning Source LLC
Chambersburg PA
CBHW061220240926
51846CB00006B/1290